PRAISE FOR

Know What You're FOR

Jeff Henderson is a world-class thinker and communicator—whether sharing his perspective from a stage, in a podcast, or now in this great book. I encourage you to think deeply about the insights Jeff shares and make the appropriate application to your organization. When applied well, these ideas will be transformational for you and your team.

Tim Tassopoulos, president and COO, Chick-fil-A, Inc.

This is a wonderful book—an invitation for your life and work to be rooted in a purpose beyond yourself. Jeff Henderson brings both inspiration and instruction. Read this book not just for your sake but for the sake of others.

John Ortberg, senior pastor of Menlo Church
and author of *Eternity Is Now in Session*

Jeff Henderson is the real deal. I have long admired the way he leads, and this book does not disappoint.

Mark Batterson, *New York Times* bestselling author of *The Circle Maker* and lead pastor of National Community Church

Leading my organization well is always on my mind. So this well-written and timely resource couldn't have come at a better time in my life and ministry. Jeff Henderson has encouraged me to not only care for and love well the people I work with, but also to care for myself—the one often forgotten in the shuffle of everyday life and demands. This is the book you've been waiting for if you'd like to take your team to places you've never been while living a beautiful life in the process.

Lysa TerKeurst, #1 *New York Times* bestselling author and president of Proverbs 31 Ministries

One of the lessons I've taught Jeff Henderson over the years is, "Don't get angry; get smart." That's what he teaches in his book—the powerful strategy of being FOR people, not against people. It's one of the ways we can all change the world.

Ambassador Andrew Young, former United States ambassador to the United Nations, two-time mayor of Atlanta, and civil rights leader

When your customers know you are truly for them, they will go all in for you—and bring friends. *Know What You're FOR* will position your organization for continual growth by serving people better. Exactly as Jeff says, this isn't just a good strategy for work; it's an even better strategy for *life*.

Michael Hyatt, *New York Times* bestselling author

Purpose *accelerates* the engagement of employees and the performance of the enterprise. This happens not by default but by design. *Know What You're FOR* gives you a proven path to demonstrate that you are FOR the people and FOR the success of the enterprise. This is the path of the courageous, humble, high-performance leader.

Cheryl Bachelder, former CEO of Popeyes Louisiana Kitchen, Inc., and author of *Dare to Serve*

Jeff Henderson's book is FOR the reader who wants to improve, to learn, and to apply important lessons in life and business. It is full of stories, anecdotes, and examples that are clear, practical, and easy to remember. Whether you're in a nonprofit or a for-profit, or you just love learning, this is a book with compelling lessons for success.

Frank Blake, former chairman and CEO of The Home Depot

One of our key values at fab'rik is WOW. We want to serve our customers so well that they stop and say, "Wow!" This is easier said than done. It's why this book is such a helpful, practical system for WOWing your customers, team, and community. As Jeff Henderson points out, when people experience you're FOR them, they return the favor.

Dana Spinola, founder and CEO of fab'rik

You've probably realized by now that the old ways don't work anymore in marketing, customer loyalty, and employee motivation. If you're wondering what's next, it's right here in Jeff Henderson's book. Not only does he brilliantly share an innovative concept, but he hands you and your company the playbook on how to create a brand-new marketing approach and company culture that will transform the way you relate to your customer, team, and even yourself. If you're looking for the future of business, this is it.

Carey Nieuwhof, author, podcaster, international speaker

Ten pages into *Know What You're FOR*, I was making a list of all of the business and ministry leaders I knew who should read this book. I want *every* leader to read this book. Jeff Henderson's insights will give you innovative ideas for your team and those you serve, as well as new, practical skills to turn those ideas into reality.

Kara Powell, PhD, executive director of the Fuller Youth Institute, and coauthor of *Growing Young and Growing With*

You gotta read this! Jeff Henderson reminds us that winning and excellence—in business and in life—is in direct proportion to how we lift and build up those around us.

Sid Mashburn, clothing designer and retailer: "The best men's store in America"—GQ

One of the secrets of great presenters is they are more FOR the audience than they are FOR themselves. This is true for organizations and their customers as well. Jeff Henderson presents a practical approach of how to grow our businesses by improving the lives of the people around us. As he points out, doing good in today's world is good for business.

Nancy Duarte, CEO of Duarte, Inc., and bestselling author

KNOW WHAT YOU'RE

FOR

KNOW WHAT YOU'RE

FOR

A Growth Strategy for Work,
An Even Better Strategy for Life

JEFF HENDERSON

ZONDERVAN®

ZONDERVAN

Know What You're FOR
Copyright © 2019 by Jeff Henderson

Requests for information should be addressed to:
Zondervan, *3900 Sparks Dr. SE, Grand Rapids, Michigan 49546*

ISBN 978-0-310-35631-8 (hardcover)

ISBN 978-0-310-35634-9 (audio)

ISBN 978-0-310-35633-2 (ebook)

Published in association with the literary agency of The FEDD Agency, Inc.,
Post Office Box 341973, Austin, TX 78734.

Cover design: Extra Credit Projects
Cover photo: Tarzhanova / iStock
Interior design: Kait Lamphere
Interior images: All images courtesy of Jeff Henderson, unless otherwise noted

Printed in the United States of America

19 20 21 22 23 24 LSC 10 9 8 7 6 5 4 3 2 1

To Wendy—
for believing

CONTENTS

Foreword *by John Maxwell* 16

Prologue 20

SECTION 1: FOR THE CUSTOMER

1. If a Business Was a Person 35
2. Two Questions That Cause a Business to Grow . 47
3. Keep the Main Thing the Main Thing 59
4. Become a Fan 74
5. Customer Engagement Is the
   New Customer Service 80
6. Small Is the New Big 93
7. The Social Loop 104

SECTION 2: FOR THE TEAM

8. In Favor Of 125
9. Designing a FOR Culture 130
10. Where Innovation Lives . . . or Dies 133
11. How to Create a Positive Team Culture 138
12. How to Have Better Meetings 148
13. Where the Best Ideas Are Hiding 153
14. A Vision Worth Working FOR 157

SECTION 3: FOR THE COMMUNITY

15. Good for Goodness' Sake. 171
16. The Pathway to Brand Loyalty 177
17. How to Build a Digital Community. 191

SECTION 4: FOR YOU

18. Remain Inspired. 209
19. Seven Ways to Improve You, Inc. 216
Epilogue 234

Afterword *by Andy Stanley*. 238
Acknowledgments 241

Bonus Section

Personal Brand Assessment 246
Find Your Voice Assessment. 247
A Weekly Guide to Social Media. 248
The Four for FOR Assessment 249

Notes 251

The secret of man's being is not only to live but to have something to live for.

Fyodor Dostoevsky

FOREWORD

Whenever I write a book, it's always for the same person. You. The reader.

That's because all books are for the reader's benefit—not the author's. (Despite what some authors think.) Ideally, every book I write answers a question or two that someone, somewhere, is asking about leadership, relationships, attitude, or how to do something. I've done that now for more than eighty books, and it's worked pretty well.

Turns out that being FOR people is a great way to build success.

And that's exactly the point of the book you're holding. Jeff Henderson wants to teach you the deceptively simple yet dramatically challenging concept of "know what you're FOR." It's a book about purpose, yes, but also about engagement, connection, and putting people first.

I've known Jeff for a while, and one of the most amazing things about him is how his mind works. He's wired to think of other people first. Maybe that's because of his marketing background, or perhaps it's because of his work as a minister, but whatever the source, the result of his thinking is a lifetime spent adding value to others.

I can relate. That's my life's purpose too. In fact, I know I exist to add value to leaders who multiply value to people. It's taken me forty years to hone a lifetime of work into one phrase, but that one phrase animates me like nothing else.

That's why I *love* Jeff's book. It's all about adding value to people—clients, vendors, teammates, and ourselves. Everything that you and I do as leaders in business or in the community is about people, and the people we serve are constantly asking three questions of us and our organizations:

1. Do you like me?
2. Can you help me?
3. Can I trust you?

If you look closely, you'll see that the first two questions have nothing to do with you or me and everything to do with the people we desire to serve. People want to know they matter. People want to know we are FOR them.

Jeff's book is full of great ideas to help turn your thinking in that direction. In fact, even though this is kind of taboo for a foreword (you're supposed to stir up interest for the book, not give pieces of it away), I want to share some of Jeff's best lines on his FOR philosophy:

- [Businesses] have to understand the greatest source of their credibility isn't the brand—it's the customers of the brand.
- Before we can build a business, we must build a community.
- The larger you can draw your circle of influence, the wider your potential impact spreads.

- We don't do business with people we don't trust. At least not for long.
- Information is important. But inspiration is always better.

Aren't those amazing? And the book is *full* of these kind of thoughts. It's really a must-read for anyone who wants to build a business or organization that's successful. And Jeff knows success. His time with Chick-fil-A and North Point Ministries has provided him with a front-row seat to some of the most FOR-oriented leaders in the world.

Now *you* get to benefit as well—because Jeff Henderson means what he says.

He's FOR you. And so am I.

That's why I enthusiastically recommend you read this book from cover to cover, mark it up with your thoughts and ideas, and then put everything you have into living a life FOR others.

My friend, you'll never regret it.

PROLOGUE

Most of what we've been taught about marketing is presumptuous.

Self-centered.

Soulless.

As if the goal is to interrupt someone's life by seeing who can shout the loudest and command the most attention.

Delaying a YouTube video with a five-second ad doesn't create an emotional bond with a customer, especially when the ad, unlike the video, never has trouble buffering.

Much like an uninvited dinner guest who shows up inquiring about the menu, it's all a bit rude, pretentious, emotionally unaware.

And it's no longer working.

At least not like it used to, and it's only going to get worse.

Or, actually, better.

You see, there's a new way, a better way.

It's been here the whole time, like most fundamental truths that for a season are lost. We need to find that truth again, to become reacquainted with a better way.

A way that doesn't want to take but strives to add.

A way that benefits both Wall Street and Main Street.

A way that is less concerned about creating fans and more about becoming a fan.

It's about treating customers not as algorithms but as people.

It's no longer telling people how great our products are and why we're better than our competitors.

It's about something far deeper, more profound. More substantial.

The thriving organizations of the future will find this way and walk the path. They will stand for something bigger than keeping the business alive. When this happens, organizations no longer have to worry about staying alive. That responsibility shifts to the customer—one they'll gladly take on.

When customers realize an organization is truly for them, they return the favor.

It doesn't require shouting. It doesn't require interruptions. It doesn't require demeaning the competition.

Those ways, thankfully, are fading away.

A new way is emerging, one that is better for the world around you, and for you.

It's a better strategy for work.

And an even better strategy for life.

It's what happens when you build an organization around who you're FOR.

It's what happens when you build your life around it as well.

In a hypercritical, cynical world, one that is often known for what it's against, let's be a group of people known for who and what we're FOR.

In a nutshell, that's what this book is about. It's the journey ahead. It's a community of people who want to build, not tear down.

If that describes you, and I have a feeling it does, welcome to FOR.

Driving Mr. Cathy

I was driving around town with a billionaire.

There were only two of us in the car. One of us had our 401(k) fully funded—about a billion times over. One of us didn't. One of us had invented the chicken sandwich. One of us hadn't. This explains the 401(k) discrepancies.

I don't often drive famous billionaires around. The only other time this had happened was, well, never.

I'm not sure what your experience has been driving these folks around, but I found myself driving slower, more cautiously. I could see the headlines if I somehow caused a wreck or scene. I didn't want that to be my fifteen minutes of fame.

Hands at ten and two. Eyes on the road.

My passenger was Truett Cathy, founder of Chick-fil-A, the inventor of the chicken sandwich and at that time my boss's boss's boss. I was driving Truett to a speaking engagement. I can't remember where we were going or even how I got the keys to a white Ford with cow spots on it. But here we were. The only cow-spotted car driving down the road as others passed us by with a wave or a smile.

Remember, eyes on the road. Hands at ten and two. Slow down, Jeff. Slow down.

I didn't know it at the time, but this car ride would follow me for years. I've talked about it from time to time. In looking back, I'm glad I drove slower. It allowed more time just to talk. Looking back on this drive is like putting on a pair of jeans and discovering you have a $20 bill in your pocket. It's a gift, a surprise. You smile. *Today's going to be a good day. I'm $20 ahead already.*

What surprised me about our conversation wasn't that Truett asked questions; it was the kind of questions he asked me. Remember, he's the boss. I work for him. Surely, we're going to talk about the business. Sales. Chicken. But no. We talked about . . . me. And not the surface level, "How are you doing?" with a quick transition to "Let's talk about the business." He was actually interested in me. He wanted to know how Wendy and the kids were doing. He asked about my mom and dad. We talked about parenting, about being a great husband. We talked about things of permanence. I drove slower.

One of my favorite parts of life is when unsuspecting moments become unforgettable memories. I love Disney World—but you walk into the Magic Kingdom expecting (and paying for) the memories.

I love the moments that catch you by surprise—moments you don't recognize at the time. Humble moments that take their time. They quietly make their way through the crowded thoughts, experiences, and memories in your brain, and before you know it, they're standing beside you. At some point, you turn and recognize how this moment became a memory and how it has been shaping you the whole time.

My car ride with Truett Cathy was one such moment. The questions he asked and his willingness to listen planted a seed in me. I realized that Truett was FOR me. He was more interested in what he could do FOR me than in what I could do FOR him.

Eventually it dawned on me. This was the counterintuitive process he used to grow the business. Here's how:

Truett was more interested in the business growing people than he was in people growing the business. And that's exactly how his business grew.

When you are FOR the people in and around your business, the people in and around your business become FOR you. This may sound altruistic, but I believe it is the way of the future for businesses and organizations going forward. I also believe it can help deal with a fundamental issue every organization fears—declining sales and momentum.

If you are currently experiencing a decline in sales or momentum, this book is written for you. If you ever fear a decline in sales or momentum, this book is written for you. If you are experiencing a decline in participation in a nonprofit organization, this book is written for you as well. And if you're experiencing a decline in momentum or growth personally, this book is for you too.

FOR is about growing the business and the people in the business—and that, of course, includes you. What we're going to discover is that growing, improving organizations are full of growing, improving people. Growth is a nonnegotiable. Without it, bad things happen.

Healthy things grow.

Unhealthy things die.

I believe the world needs healthier, growing businesses. I believe the world needs more thriving nonprofit organizations. And within both, I believe we need more thriving, growing people.

It's why the car ride with Truett clued me in on one of his secrets to growing his business. Over time, I've boiled the secret down to two questions. Sure, there are plenty of reasons and factors that cause an organization to grow. However, if you forced me to describe growth in a simple way that everyone can understand, I'll point you to the two questions we're going to reveal in this book. My experience is that these two questions are the catalyst for growth in businesses, organizations, and people. It's where purpose and action meet.

For example, when a business leverages the power of the two questions in this book, it harnesses the greatest form of advertising the world has ever seen—positive word-of-mouth advertising.

It's why, if you want your business or nonprofit to grow, the answers to these two questions must match. When the team of any organization understands these two questions and what their roles are to make them match, momentum is bound to follow. It's not easy, but it is simple.

This is going to require us to rethink our business approach. I believe businesses can make a profit *and* improve the world. However, our approach to marketing and messaging needs to change. Instead of shouting about how great the business is, we need to start talking about how great our customers are and engage with them about their life.

Thriving businesses will practice less monologue and more dialogue.

In today's world, if a CEO is riding in a car with a customer, the primary topic of conversation will be about the business. "Have you seen our new product?" "Did you see our latest offer?" "Did you see we are better and cheaper than our competitor?"

In other words, it's all about the business. It's all monologue. But customers are walking away from that kind of approach.

The thriving businesses of tomorrow will take a different approach. Instead of talking about the business, the CEO will ask different questions. Far less about the business. Far more about the customer. "How are you?" "What are *your* dreams, *your* hopes?" "How can we help?"

If this sounds obvious, trust me. It's not. In the first section of the book, I'll prove it. When I present this concept to business leaders, they lean back and say, "Jeff, we already do this. We engage and talk with our customers about them." Then, with one click of a button, I show them something about their business that is the complete opposite of what they just said. Their usual response is, "Oh, wow." Sometimes the three-letter word *wow* is replaced with a four-letter word, but who's counting?

The reason I've written this book is to help your business or nonprofit organization grow. Yes, that growth definitely includes sales and momentum, but it's even better than that. You can grow sales and value—real human value. You can grow the business by growing the people in your business. And in the process, you grow too.

You do this by being FOR people. You do this by helping people move closer to their potential. To be more FOR them than you are FOR yourself.

IN today's world, what's good for people is good for business.

It's a fantastic strategy for business.

More importantly, it's a fantastic strategy for life.

The beautiful part is you don't have to pick between those two. In today's world, what's good for people is good for business.

Four for FOR

To get there, here's where we're going. Once we've established the two questions your organization needs to ask and answer, we're going to provide practical strategies you can implement to be FOR the people in your business.

For an organization to grow there are four groups to be FOR:

- the customer
- the team
- the community
- and you

When you are FOR these people, you create a combustible engine where positive word-of-mouth advertising is generated. When you are FOR these people, they return the favor. And yes, you are one of the four. I'll show you how being FOR you is actually one of the best ways to be FOR the other three. It's why this book will not only grow your organization; it will also grow you and your influence as well.

To get there, here's a brief road map of where we're going:

1. FOR the Customer

One of the primary ways a business grows is by creating a sales force for free. Everyone understands the value of positive word-of-mouth advertising. The problem is that it seems so elusive, even mysterious. We're going to take the mystery out of it by giving you a very practical strategy for engaging with your customers.

In this section, we'll introduce a relatively new form of customer engagement that very few brands, businesses, and organizations are leveraging. If you are interested in creating positive word-of-mouth advertising, this section will lead you there.

2. FOR the Team

An organization cannot create a healthy customer culture with an unhealthy team culture. When a team understands the organization and leadership are FOR them, they return the favor. One of the most important lessons we can't afford to forget in any business is this: A customer is treated like the team is treated. For example, when I walk into a business, I can instantly tell how the team is being treated. It is flowing to me and the other customers.

One of the ways an organization accomplishes this is by having a clear, compelling vision that closes the gap between the two questions we're going to look at in this book.

We are also going to provide practical ways for you to reinforce the vision of your organization. As we'll see, *vision rarely repeated is quickly forgotten*.

But it's not just about the vision of the organization. It's about the vision you have for the team. People want to work for someone who clearly wants and believes the best in them. A business with a FOR mind-set understands that the first customer a leader has is *the team*. Too often, we try to solve this with off-site retreats. I'm all for off-sites, but they are often seen as a magic pill—the performance-enhancing steroid of organizational life.

Creating a culture where your team knows you are FOR them and they are FOR one another takes more time and intentionality than that. In this section, we are going to provide practical tips on how to make this happen. For example, let's take one of the most unpopular parts of any organizational life—meetings. (Does anything in our work lives take more criticism than this?) Generally speaking, we all hate meetings. And yet, with a simple shift in our meeting preparation, we can leverage the time and create a FOR culture that turns often wasted time into leveraged time.

3. FOR the Community

It's no longer enough to be the best company IN the world. It's about being the best company FOR the world.

This is going to require having a bigger purpose than just "staying in business." When businesses have a "bigger than us" mentality and see community impact as a measurement of business success, you are well on your way toward a purpose that rallies and inspires.

IT'S no longer enough to be the best company IN the world. It's about being the best company FOR the world.

This is more than a volunteer service project once a year though. Being for your community requires a consistent, systematic, and sustainable process with both messaging and operations. The primary reason you rally around people in your community isn't to get them to do business with you. You rally around the people in your community because, well, they are people in your community.

In this section, we'll provide practical ways for your organization to show you are FOR your community. It's not advertising. It's real.

4. FOR You

This section is focused on the one person you have the most control over—you. Honestly, you're probably the only person you have any real control over.

In order to breathe healthy life into the organization, you must ensure you're breathing it in first. The best gift you can give your customers, your team, and your community is an inspired, rejuvenated, fully alive you.

It's why this section is FOR you. One of the best ways this

book can help your customers, team, and community is to help you. The first three will require a lot of output from you in terms of energy, creativity, and leadership. If we're not careful, we'll wake up one day with very little to give. That's a loss for all four. In this section, you'll find practical tips on how to give the people in your organization the best you. Additionally, you will find in the bonus section links to free assessments, such as a personal branding survey and the Four Presenter Voices helping you discover your presentation voice, along with an assessment for your organization. All of this is designed to help you and your career. After all, we need a healthy you.

It's why FOR isn't just a better strategy for work; it's also a better strategy for life.

When these four groups grow—customers, team, community, and leaders—the organization grows as a result, even in the most challenging of situations.

My passenger in the car could tell you all about challenging situations. One of his most challenging was in 1982, when Chick-fil-A was facing new competitors, skyrocketing inflation, and the completion of a new $10 million corporate headquarters. That's a lot of pressure riding on a chicken sandwich with two pickles.

In this challenging situation, Truett decided to do something that I'm going to challenge you to do—to clarify who he and the organization were FOR. I'm going to walk you through two questions to get us there and then apply it to the Four for FOR. By doing this, you will grow the business by growing the people in your business.

This isn't theory. I've seen it. I've experienced it. I've been the recipient of it. I have had the privilege of working for two thriving organizations at the top of their fields—Chick-fil-A and North Point Ministries. A few years ago, I realized it wasn't just a blessing to work for these organizations. I had a stewardship responsibility to pass along what I had learned.

What caused them to grow? Are there similar principles that every organization can harness and apply to cause them to grow as well? I've discovered that there are, and that's where we're going in the journey ahead.

One of the lessons we'll learn is that when your business is authentically FOR people, people will become authentically FOR the business. I've seen this not only in the business world but also in the nonprofit world, and I've even seen it in a car with cow spots, driving around town with a billionaire.

It's time for a new way—a way that impacts both brick-and-mortar and online stores. A way that grows the business by growing people. A way that builds the best organizations FOR the world.

So buckle up. Here we go.

But don't be concerned. I'm driving slow. Ten and two. Eyes on the road.

FOR THE CUSTOMER

IF A BUSINESS
Was a Person

Most social media posts of a business are 99.9 percent about the business. Most advertising is as well. And the same could be said of churches and nonprofits.

"Look at our products." "New sermon series starting Sunday!" "Buy one, get one free!"

The focus is clearly on the business, by the business, for the business.

This has been the case for so long that it's sometimes hard to see the danger in this. But the danger's there, and it's only growing.

Here's why: If a business was a person, many businesses would be considered narcissists. And narcissism is bad for business.

The definition of a narcissist is "a person who has an excessive interest in or admiration of themselves." And to pile on, Google drives home the point further: "Narcissists are those who think the world revolves around them."

> **IF a business was a person, many businesses would be considered narcissists. And narcissism is bad for business.**

I bet narcissism never came up in business school, did it?

It's why you may be tempted to dismiss this notion and stop reading. Before you do, at least make it to chapter 4. And please understand two important distinctions:

1. I'm not saying the people in your organization are narcissists.
2. I'm suggesting we've been taught to shine the spotlight on the organization and not the customer.

I'm often called on to consult with religious organizations and nonprofits. Imagine how this goes over when I talk about this with church leaders. "Wait, what? You're saying my church is narcissistic?"

"No," I'll reply, "I'm suggesting it is displaying narcissistic tendencies."

Before I'm kicked out of the building, we do a quick exercise by visiting the Instagram page of their church. I ask them to count how many of the last ten posts are about the church and how many are about the community or people outside the four walls of the church. Usually, it's nine to one in favor of the church. Honestly, more often than not, it's ten to zero.

In other words, the spotlight is clearly on the church and not the community.

The business world is no different.

Thriving businesses and nonprofit organizations of the future will understand the danger of this. And when I say *future*, I'm not suggesting fifteen years from now.

The future is here. The organizations that understand this and shift the focus from the business to the customer will win the heart of the customer. And the heart of the customer is the great battleground. When you do this effectively, customers start talking positively. They notice you are FOR them. In turn, they become FOR you. It's as if they have a personal, vested interest in supporting the business. They become your sales force . . . for free. This is the fertile ground where positive word-of-mouth advertising begins to grow.

In this new world, online reviews win out over paid advertising. Brands that advertise how great they are lack credibility. As Scott Cook, cofounder of Intuit and a billionaire director of both Procter and Gamble and eBay, correctly points out, "A brand is no longer what it tells consumers it is—it is what consumers tell each other it is."[1]

For this to happen, you must give them a reason to say yes to the following question.

A Question Your Customer Is Asking about You

One of my business heroes is Horst Schulze. Mr. Schulze is the chairman and chief executive officer at Capella Hotels and Resorts and Solis Hotels and Resorts.

He cofounded the Ritz-Carlton. During his time there, the Ritz-Carlton won the prestigious Malcolm Baldridge National Quality Award for exemplary customer service, not once, but twice.

This kind of compelling and exemplary service is built on a question. This single question drives the systems, focus, and, yes, heart of the business.

"The number one question customers are asking about a business is, 'Do they care about me?'" Mr. Schulze says.

It's so easy to dismiss this question. It seems touchy-feely. It seems hard to measure. And no one would admit out loud that they don't care about the customer.

If you look closer, though, you'll find systems that have a natural bent toward spotlighting and protecting the business.

A great example is the banking industry. While online banking has made a significant shift in how banks interact with their customers, there is still the occasional need to actually go inside a branch. Typically, you'll find a queue line, and then when it's your turn, the branch employee will say, "Next."

"How many of you," Mr. Schulze will ask his audiences, "are named 'Next'?"

One of the greatest sounds we like to hear is when someone says our name. "Hey, buddy" often sounds like, "You don't know my name." "Hey, Jeff" creates a much better feeling and emotion when I hear it. I bet the same is true with you.

It's why the Ritz-Carlton built a system around getting to know your name and spreading it to the rest of their team during your stay. When they say your name, it shows they care.

Several years in a row, my daughter and I would attend a father-daughter dance. (Honestly, I would still like to do this, but Jesse is in college now, and for some reason she has declined. I still ask every year though.)

One year, I decided we would stay at the Ritz-Carlton in Buckhead, a few minutes north of downtown Atlanta. I was the lead pastor of Buckhead Church. Our church was very close to the Ritz.

Jesse was eight years old at the time. When we arrived, the Ritz-Carlton team helped us get our bags out of the car. The first thing they did, though, was to introduce themselves and ask for our names. (Note: this is a system.)

They asked us to proceed to the registration desk, where they would meet us with our bags. As we were walking in, I glanced back to see the bellman whispering into his shirtsleeve, like he was in the Secret Service. (Note: this is another system.)

Quick question—what was he doing? Why was he whispering into his sleeve?

It all goes back to a question that customers ask: "Does this business really care about me?" And nothing quite communicates care than when a customer hears a business say their name.

As Jesse and I walked into the beautiful Ritz-Carlton Buckhead and approached the registration desk, we were greeted with, "Good evening, Mr. Henderson and Jesse. We are so glad you're here."

I wish you could have seen Jesse's eyes. The memory of that moment brings a smile to my face and tears to my eyes as I write this. When we were walking to our room, Jesse whispered to me, "Dad, how did they know our names?"

I smiled and said, "Honey, your dad is big-time in Buckhead."

That was eleven years ago. I remember it like it was yesterday. Heck, in some ways, it feels like yesterday. I tell that story often. I never tell the stories of the times I was called "Next."

This doesn't happen by accident. It happens with a fundamental decision to create systems that are FOR the customer.

Let's rewind the tape and reveal what happened. As Jesse and I drove up, the bellman knew his most important job wasn't just helping us with our bags; his most important job was discovering our names. Once he had our names, he went Secret

Service on us by radioing to the front desk. "Mr. Henderson and his daughter, Jesse."

The person at the desk heard it, confirmed it over the radio with the bellman, and was ready with a smile and our names. And here we are, eleven years later, and I'm still telling that story.

Did Jesse and I think the Ritz-Carlton cared about us? Well, of course. They knew our names. And as Norm from *Cheers* will tell you, we all want to go "where everybody knows your name."

What's most impressive to me about this is that it required planning. It required thinking through a system that could be replicated throughout the entire Ritz-Carlton chain. Somewhere at some time, a team of people sat down and said, "How can we capture the names of our guests and repeat it back to them within thirty seconds of their arrival?"

This is what it means to be FOR your customer. To not only say we care, but to make specific, systematic shifts toward showing it. When this happens, customers respond. They tell others about it, and you begin to reap the pixie dust of advertising called word-of-mouth. But you have to give customers something to say. Taking their bags is expected. Learning and saying their names is a Wow. When this happens, we show customers we care. And this is great for business growth because every customer is asking a question about your organization: "Do they care about me?"

And people respond to organizations that truly care for them.

What Causes a Business to Grow?

Every day when businesses, churches, and nonprofit organizations open their doors, some type of growth is the goal. It could be an increase in customers, sales, or membership, or personal or spiritual growth, but ultimately every organization needs to grow. Healthy things grow. Unhealthy things die.

No one ever started an organization and said, "One day I hope this organization dies."

Growth may look different, but it's something we all should want. Knowing this, what causes a business to grow? Sure, there are lots of answers, but ultimately it comes down to one word—*customers*.

We must learn to care more for the customer than we care for the business. We must learn to care more about people than about the organization. This isn't bad for business because customers *are* the business. Caring for the customer creates an emotional bond that allows them to care more about the business. Now, more than ever, we have an extraordinary opportunity to show customers *we* care.

Years ago, there was a commercial in which a CEO calls his team together in a meeting. He begins by addressing the downturn in sales. Then he begins handing out airline tickets. "We're going to go visit our customers, and it starts with me." He shows them his ticket, puts on his coat, and walks out the door.

We don't have to wait for a downturn. We can implement specific systems to show customers we do truly care about them. This is true for large organizations, start-ups, and small ones. A great example of this is Jan Smith. In fact, in her story, her clients gave Jan a nickname for how much she cared.

Justin Bieber and Mama Jan

Maybe you've heard of Justin Bieber. After all, he has 104 million followers on Twitter. When you reach this level of fame and stardom, history tells us that "yes people" begin to surface.

Everything a superstar says or does is usually applauded or affirmed because that's where the money flows.

It's why Jan Smith's approach is so refreshing. Jan owns a vocal coaching business in Atlanta called Jan Smith Studios. She grew up as a musician herself and recorded her first album at the age of fifteen. Years later, Jan was asked if she could help a musician who was losing his voice. In the span of a few coaching sessions, she helped turn not only his voice around but his life as well.

"It was so cool because I immediately saw the impact of helping someone," Jan said. "That led to another client, which led to another, which led to forty and then seventy. Then I trained a client to help coach more through her. *I began to realize the more I helped people, the more the business grew.*"[2]

Fast-forward to today, Jan and her team coach more than two hundred people a week. And while the business has grown, one thing has remained the same: she shoots straight with her clients.

If you want a yes-man around you, don't hire Jan Smith. If you want someone to be more FOR you than they are for their business, Jan Smith is the one you hire as your coach. Don't take my word for it. Take Justin Bieber's. Or talk to Usher, Rob Thomas, Shania Twain, The Band Perry. You could even talk to actor Dwayne "The Rock" Johnson. The list goes on and on.

"Honesty and authenticity," says Jan, "are so important. I'm going to tell them the truth. I don't really care if my honesty negatively impacts my business. I think they understand that I love them as a person more than I do as a client. If they mess up, they know I'm going to tell them. If I tell them their performance was really good, then they know it was really good. I'm honest."

Which is exactly what I saw when my family spent one Friday evening at home watching the Justin Bieber documentary *Never Say Never*. I'll be honest, both my son and I voiced some initial complaints about this movie choice, but it was my daughter's turn to decide on a movie, so we abided by the family rules. Immediately we were drawn into the story. It was a fascinating inside look at how Justin's fame reached meteoric levels due to his talent and the team around him, including Scooter Braun and Jan Smith.

Halfway through the documentary, guess who I see? My friend Jan Smith. I knew she coached Justin. I just didn't know she was in the movie. And right there, in front of all the world to see, you saw Jan Smith being honest with one of the most famous people on the planet.

Based on the pace of the concerts, Justin was on the verge of losing his voice. Canceling concerts to save his voice would be a very difficult decision because of the amount of money involved. It wasn't difficult at all for Jan Smith.

"Justin," she said, "you need to rest your voice. We need to cancel."

And that's what happened.

As a result of this kind of honesty and care that Jan has for her clients, they began to give her a nickname—Mama Jan.

"How I got to be Mama Jan is funny to me," she said. "I don't have children of my own. I think my clients call me Mama because they know I love them. The truth is so important in this business because the more famous someone becomes, the harder it is to discern truth because people are attaching themselves to you for all sorts of reasons. They are going to say what they think you want to hear. I love my clients. God put a big heart in me. Regardless of what goes down, I'm going to be there. If any of my clients, famous or not, need me at 2:00 a.m., they know they can call me.

"They also know I'm willing to lose their business by being honest and authentic with them. I care more about them than I care about having their business."[3]

Remember how I described Truett Cathy and his approach to a business?

Truett was more interested in the business growing people than he was in people growing the business. And that's exactly how his business grew.

This is exactly how Jan grew her business as well. She is more interested in *growing her clients than growing her client base.* There's a significant difference between the two. This is what it means to be FOR your clients and customers.

But don't miss the power of this. It doesn't mean growing the business or organization is wrong. Far from it. Don't forget, growth is what we're going for in this book. What we're talking about is the emphasis of *where the growth happens* and *where it begins.*

What causes a business or organization to grow? Well, here are the three causes:

1. When our focus is on growing people, people grow the business.
2. When we think more about how the business can help and serve people, the more people we will eventually help and serve.
3. When we think more about the customer than we do the business, it is the best way we can think about the

business. When we're thinking about our customer, we ARE thinking about the business.

It all sounds so simple, and the good news is it really is. The problem is getting back to simple. The challenge is moving against the natural tendency to drift toward thinking more about the organization than thinking about the customer. At some point, the hidden, secret goal of any organization is survival. It's why change is often so hard to implement. When the goal of the organization is survival, it sounds like, "That's not how we do it around here."

WHEN the goal of the organization is survival, it sounds like, "That's not how we do it around here."

One of the best ways to implement change isn't for change's sake. It's to stay current, relevant, and honest with your customer. It's why we must take an honest, hard look at our operational systems, marketing, and messaging. The drift is always toward what's best for the organization and how to tell our story. Sure, there's a place to tell our story, but remember, our story isn't the most important one. The most important story is the one about our customer. When our story supports the customer's story, they begin to share that story.

It's why it's important to examine the focus of our social media, advertising, and messaging. The focus of a company's social media is a clue as to where most of the systems are pointing—either to highlighting the business or highlighting the customer.

Is it wrong to spotlight your business or church on social media?

Of course not.

Is it wrong to spotlight your business far more than you do your customer?

It all depends on how you answer the questions in the next chapter—the two questions that cause a business to grow.

TWO QUESTIONS
That Cause a Business
TO GROW

I began my marketing career working for the Atlanta Braves, where I learned there's nothing quite like winning to boost ticket sales, no matter how many cool bobblehead promotions you can create. After working in marketing for Callaway Gardens and Lake Lanier Islands Resorts, I joined Chick-fil-A, where I helped lead the sports and beverage marketing efforts.

When I left Chick-fil-A to join North Point Ministries, I went from one thriving organization to another. In 2018, Chick-fil-A generated more than $10 billion in sales, marking fifty-one years of consecutive same-store sales growth. With more than 2,300 locations in forty-six states, I would say Chick-fil-A knows a thing or two about growth. North Point Ministries has been called the largest church in America by *Outreach Magazine*. Each week, more than thirty thousand people attend a North Point campus in the Atlanta area. Each month, sermons and leadership messages are accessed more than one million times through their websites.

All that said, you could argue that Chick-fil-A and North

Point are at the top of their fields. I've been blessed to work for and learn from both.

As a result, one of the questions I'm often asked is, "What is the biggest difference between working at Chick-fil-A and North Point Ministries?"

That's an easy answer.

The biggest difference is I'm open on Sundays now. Chick-fil-A is not.

The better question to ask, I believe, is "What are the similarities between the two?"

I've discovered that thriving organizations have a lot more in common, even if what they do is drastically different. And one of those similarities is how they have grown their respective organizations.

What Causes a Business to Grow?

This leads to our two questions that will follow us throughout the rest of the book:

1. What do we want to be known FOR?
2. What are we known FOR?

"What do we want to be known FOR?" is our vision. It's our big idea. It's our niche, our foothold, in the marketplace. The first question is the one we answer. Here lies the purpose, the vision, the why.

"What *are* we known FOR?" is the customers' experience of our vision. It's their reflection of whether they are experiencing the purpose and vision of the organization.

The first question is what we say; the second question is what customers say.

Within these two questions is the secret to growth. When the answers to these two questions match, growth happens. It's that simple. And it's that hard.

When what you want to be known FOR is actually what you *are* known FOR, customers become a sales force for free by telling others about you.

When you have a compelling vision, product, and purpose, and customers experience it, they gladly become a source of positive word-of-mouth advertising.

WHEN what you want to be known FOR is actually what you *are* known FOR, customers become a sales force for free by telling others about you.

One of the reasons sales decline in a business is that the answers to these two questions don't match. When there is a gap in these two questions, there will be a gap in sales. Momentum slows.

The reality for every organization is that there *is* a gap. There's no perfect organization. We all have our good days and our bad days. The goal isn't perfection; the goal is *progress*. It's why the goal of every organization should be to shrink the gap between the answers to these two questions and make sure they match as consistently as possible.

That's what this book is about. Being FOR the customers, the team, the community, and you is the pathway to closing the gap between these two questions.

If you're experiencing declining sales or momentum, the good news is that you can close the gap by implementing the practices in this book. If you want to *avoid* declining sales, you can do the same as well.

The challenge is that many organizations aren't clear about what they want to be known FOR. And if the organization is confused about this, the customers most certainly will be.

By contrast, when what you want to be known FOR *is* what you are known FOR, you grow.

Here's why this is true: *the four P's of marketing are dead.*

The first day in Marketing 101, we were taught the "four P's" of marketing:

- product
- price
- place
- promotion

In his book *The Digital Economy*, author Don Tapscott explains how each of these have been replaced.[4] I think he's right.

And yet I think there was a missing "P" all along, and it's very much alive, relevant, and vital to growing any organization— most importantly, *your* organization.

It's not really the fifth "P." It's number one. It always has been, and it always will be.

Thriving organizations live and breathe this. You feel it in their DNA. It electrifies the culture with a buoyant spirit. It turns a job into a calling, a customer into a friend, a company into a movement.

If that sounds a bit dramatic, well, it's supposed to be.

For far too long, we've been taught an emotionless, staid, joyless version of business.

The thriving organizations I've been a part of and am a customer of are anything but this. It's as if they secretly believe they are in the middle of a movie script and the drama is playing out before them.

And they clearly live out the number one "P"—*purpose*.

Purpose infuses their culture in a way that product, price, place, and promotion never could.

Joey Reiman, author of *The Story of Purpose: The Path to Creating a Brighter Brand, a Greater Company, and a Lasting Legacy*, says, "Purpose is where your company's distinctive gifts intersect with the needs of the world."[5]

The problem with purpose, though, is that most organizations put a check in that box, thinking they've covered it. After all, they went on a two-day off-site four years ago and developed a mission statement. No one remembers it or can quote it—but still, we covered that four years ago.

Thriving organizations understand that purpose is too large for a one-time event. Purpose is a *daily* event. It's why you must rally everyone around these two questions. It doesn't matter if you're an entrepreneur striving to launch your idea or an intrapreneur working within an existing organization. It doesn't matter if you've been around for five years or five days.

It doesn't matter if you're a business or nonprofit organization. I've seen the power of this applied at Chick-fil-A. And I've seen the power of it during my season as a church planter.

For example, Gwinnett Church is located in North Atlanta and is a campus of North Point Ministries, which has seven campuses around the city. In 2011, we began the launch phase of the first Gwinnett location. We launched a second location in Gwinnett County in 2019.

In the start-up days of Gwinnett Church, I gathered our small team of four and began the way I would advise any business or nonprofit launcher to begin. I asked them this question: "What do we want to be known FOR?"

"What Do We Want to Be Known FOR?"

Welcome to the Land of Purpose. It's where this question lives. It's also where thriving organizations live.

If it's okay, I would like to show you how this question led Gwinnett Church to a very important place. Again, this is a business book, not a religion book. But if you can give me a few paragraphs, I want to show you how this played out for our church and how it can play out for your organization.

In a few years, Gwinnett County in north metro Atlanta will become the most populated county in the state of Georgia. It is also one of the most diverse counties in the southeastern United States. Additionally, of the ten largest high schools in the state of Georgia, eight are in Gwinnett County alone. The potential to impact people in this county is enormous.

In 2003, I left Chick-fil-A to join the early days of Buckhead Church, North Point's first multisite location. During this time, I became lead pastor and helped lead Buckhead to its current location. In 2011, my friend and boss Andy Stanley asked me to leave Buckhead to help start Gwinnett Church. In other words, I was starting all over. In a matter of a couple of Sundays, I went from serving a congregation of more than seven thousand to zero. (Well, if you counted my family, I guess you could say from seven thousand to four.)

If you've ever started something, you know the temptation is to "get to work." In other words, start running. Before we start running, though, we need to start thinking and dreaming. It's hard work, but without it you can start running toward no clear direction.

It's why, in the initial start-up days of Gwinnett Church, we had plenty of dream sessions. I love these early days of "What could be?" (Side note: Don't ever lose the early days of "What could be?" If you do, you begin to wither.)

The focus of our dream sessions always came back to this question: "What do we want to be known FOR?" During one of our dream sessions, someone said, "Many people are more familiar with what the church is against rather than what the church is FOR. We should be known for what we're FOR."

Everything stopped.

We looked at each other.

There are moments in life when you realize it's not an ordinary one. This moment was one of those for me.

"With that being the case, what do we want to be known FOR?"

And that's when it started. Everyone started talking about what we're FOR. More importantly, WHOM we are FOR.

- "We're FOR Gwinnett kids."
- "We're FOR Gwinnett businesses."
- "We're FOR Gwinnett adults."
- "We're FOR Gwinnett students."
- "We are FOR Gwinnett."
- "It's about THEM; it's not about US."

That was eight years ago. Our aim has been to stay on message from then until now. It's what we want to be known FOR.

This has been a huge rallying cry for us, providing clarity of the *why* behind the *what* for the *who*.

Okay, we can relax. Church talk is over.

Here's my point. "What do you want your organization to be known FOR?"

And before we go to the file drawer to pull out our four-paragraph mission statement, we must remind ourselves that the walk to the file drawer means no one knows what the purpose statement is that's in the file drawer.

WHEN purpose lives in an organization, the organization lives in purpose.

It's no small thing that sixteen years after working for Chick-fil-A, I can still easily recite their corporate purpose statement. It's no small thing that I can do the same with North Point Ministries.

When purpose lives in an organization, the organization lives in purpose.

Delivering Happiness

A few years ago, I had the opportunity to tour the headquarters of Zappos near Las Vegas. If you haven't heard of Zappos, you should check them out. They are quite the success story, going from zero to $1 billion in sales of shoes and apparel in only ten years. Eventually, they were bought by Amazon, like we all will be one day.

Zappos CEO Tony Hsieh has done an amazing job of creating clarity and focus around the answer to the question, "What do we want to be known FOR?" Tony wanted Zappos to be known for delivering happiness more than delivering shoes.

Delivering happiness is not one of the core tenets taught in business school. After all, how do you measure happiness on a spreadsheet?

But Tony knew that what most people want is happiness. If Zappos could deliver happiness while delivering shoes, people might just end up ordering more of both, and happiness *would* actually end up on a spreadsheet.

He was right. In fact, happiness measured up to $1 billion . . . and still counting.

When I visited Zappos, guess what I observed? Happiness. As usual, it starts with the team and flows from there. It's impossible to deliver happiness to customers without first delivering it to your team. (More on that later.)

I was led to where happiness was delivered—not a warehouse, but the call center. This is where the magic happens.

Zappos prides itself on building real relationships with its customers. They believe it all comes down to relationships. Most companies say something like that on their website. Zappos tries to live it out every day.

One of the ways they accomplish this is celebrating the amount of time they spend talking to customers on the phone. Most call centers try to get you on and off the phone as soon as possible in order to get to the next customer. Not Zappos. You can't hurry real relationships. And when it comes to delivering happiness, it really does come down to relationships.

In fact, the most celebrated, legendary customer call of all time goes to the Zappos employee who spoke to a customer for six hours. That's right. Six.

Turns out this customer had just lost her husband and during the course of the conversation began to share with the Zappos employee what had happened. Six hours later, a customer had become a friend. (By the way, the customer didn't even end up purchasing shoes. That's okay. The next time that customer needs shoes, who do you think she'll call?) The most important part of this story is that the employee wasn't admonished for spending so much time on the phone and not making a sale. Instead, the employee was celebrated. Why? She was trying to deliver happiness to a customer who needed it more than shoes.

The team at Zappos is crystal clear about their answer to the question, "What do we want to be known FOR?" They sell shoes and apparel, but they want to be known for *delivering happiness*, and it's working.

How about you? What does your organization want to be known FOR?

Once you have a clear, concise, and compelling answer to this question, your next step is to connect it with the second question.

"What *Are* We Known FOR?"

The first question is for us to answer. The second question is for the customers to answer.

"What do we want to be known FOR?" is the brand promise. "What *are* we known FOR?" reveals how well we are delivering on the promise.

This is why so many organizations spend marketing dollars to their detriment. They make promises they can't keep. And we all know what happens between friends when one friend makes promises they don't keep.

When this happens, the organization loses credibility, not just with its customers, but with the team. We're talking the talk but not walking the walk. And we are leaving dollars and impact on the table.

Let's go back to Zappos. The reason they grew so fast is that they clearly answered the first question and structured their organization around delivering it in the second question. If they said "we want to deliver happiness" but then admonished a team member for spending six hours on the phone with a customer and failing to close a sale, there would be a gap. But when they celebrate that team member, they reinforce the connection between both of those questions. In other words, Zappos wants to be known for delivering happiness, and that has been reflected back to them by their customers. They made a brand promise of "delivering happiness," and then they created systems to deliver that brand promise.

All of that leads me to this: In order to ensure consistent growth, the goal of *everyone* in the organization should be to make the answers to "What do we want to be known FOR?" and "What *are* we known FOR?" match.

This is also the most important challenge for any leader.

When there is a gap between these two questions, symptoms of decline will appear. It may look like a disengaged staff, inconsistent customer ratings, and declining sales. That's not the real problem though. It's deeper than that.

The organization is drifting. There is no anchor. There aren't systems delivering the brand promise. On the other hand, when the answers to these questions match, great symptoms begin to appear. Employees understand why they do what they do. Customers experience the brand promise. As a result, they tell others about it. You create a sales force for free, harnessing the power of word-of-mouth advertising.

And the organization grows.

When these two questions connect, you experience the number one "P" in marketing—PURPOSE. And there's nothing quite like purpose to consistently grow your business.

Accomplishing this isn't easy, but the good news is that it's simple. When everyone is clear on the brand promise and how we are currently achieving that brand promise, purpose will grow. Momentum will follow. And sales will too.

The challenge is how do we get there?

That's what this book is all about. It's why I hope this isn't a one-time read, but a reference for your organization's journey. For example, in the bonus section of the book, you'll find a link to a free, downloadable survey that you can use within your organization. This is designed to help you measure where the gaps are between the two growth questions and how to close it.

Along those lines, another idea is to informally ask people on your team and your customers, "What *are* we known FOR?" This won't be as scientific as the survey will be, but it may give you a quick, intuitive feel for what's really happening.

Either way, the point remains. Your present challenge is to simply figure out if there is distance between these two questions, and if so, how do you shrink the gap?

One warning. This will take some time, especially if your organization has been around for a while. But when we fail to do the hard work of connecting these two questions, we shortchange ourselves, our customers, and our purpose. We choose short-term over long-term, or, in the following example, hamburgers over pancakes.

Keep the Main Thing
THE MAIN THING

CHAPTER 3

IHOB

Back in the summer of 2018, International House of Pancakes decided they wanted to be known for something else. Instead of pancakes they would now be known as International House of Burgers. Out with the *P* and in with the *B*.

They had a really clever logo change by simply turning the *p* upside down, and they received an extraordinary amount of publicity over this. It trended #1 on Twitter for quite a while.

That's the good news.

The bad news is that much of the response could be accurately summed up with a tweet from Wendy's (see next page).

I'm sure there were a lot of great reasons for the change. Customers just didn't buy it.

Wanting to be known FOR *the* place internationally for hamburgers in a world of hamburgers is ambitious, for sure. And you can't blame a business for wanting to be ambitious.

But before a business leaps toward ambition, they must ask the more grounded question: "What *are* we known FOR?" The

answer in this case is . . . pancakes. When you are known for one thing but talk about being known for something else, you lose an important value to your brand: CREDIBILITY.

My hunch is that the impetus for this name change generated from a boardroom instead of the dining room. For example, has anyone ever said to you, "If you want a great hamburger, you've got to go to International House of Pancakes"?

Yeah, me either. As a result, an announcement like this lacks credibility. And when you hurt your brand's credibility, you hurt your brand.

In today's fast-paced world that demands immediate results, it's easy to fall into the temptation of logo changes and big announcements. And to be fair, it works for a while. But here's the challenge: Are you really the place for the greatest hamburgers in the world? Will people from France come to the

United States, get off the plane, and ask the Uber driver, "Take me to this IHOB."

Will Buddy the Elf walk into IHOB and shout, "You did it! You created the best hamburger in the world!"

Customers are savvier than Buddy the Elf. The better play here would have been to let customers announce the change. "I always just thought of IHOP for breakfast," Bob said, "but one day I went there for lunch and had the hamburger. That's when I thought, *I think this might be the greatest hamburger in the world!*"

Multiply Bob by hundreds, and you might be onto something.

If there are no Bobs, then it comes off as a marketing gimmick. And marketing gimmicks don't last. Brands that chase after them often don't either.

Granted, I could be wrong. If I am, send me an email and let me know how great the burgers are at IHOB—jeff@theforcompany.com.

I'm waiting.

AN EXERCISE FOR YOUR NEXT TEAM MEETING

I certainly hope I'm not coming across too harsh to IHOP. (I'm sorry—IHOB.)

But brands like this have to understand the greatest source of their credibility isn't the brand; it's the customers of the brand.

When customers tell customers about the hamburgers at IHOP, then you can change it to IHOB.

This isn't easy. That's why organizations need great leaders like you. It's why I think the remaining chapters of *Know What You're FOR* can help you get there.

To prepare you for that, I have a few items for the agenda at your next team meeting:

1. Ask each team member to identify one of their favorite companies, and why it's one of their favorites.
2. Then ask them what's the one thing that company is known FOR.
3. How are they delivering on their brand promise?
4. Transition the conversation to your organization by asking, "What are *we* known FOR?"
5. Follow this by asking, "What do we *want* to be known FOR?"
6. Finish the meeting by identifying gaps between these two questions.

A Cure to Insider-itis

The challenge with the sixth agenda item in the team exercise is that we potentially see the gaps with blinders on. There are gaps we don't often see because it's hidden within the confines of our own knowledge and experience. I call it insider-itis.

Insider-itis is a made-up term that spell-check hates. But it is alive and well, dangerously so, in many organizations.

Insider-itis is a malady afflicting the vision of organizations by focusing on insider issues over outsider issues. "This is how we've always done it" becomes the mantra over "What are we learning from our customers in order to better serve them?"

The future is going to reward businesses and organizations that are designed to see the world from the customer's perspective. It sounds easy. It's far from it.

INSIDER-ITIS is a malady afflicting the vision of organizations by focusing on insider issues over outsider issues.

For example, when I worked with Chick-fil-A, I served individual restaurant operators to help build their sales. One example of this is a full one-day marketing makeover. The primary focus of this day is to see the business from the customer's perspective. One of the ways we did this was during lunch, the busiest time of the day. Usually and understandably, the operators would find themselves behind the counter serving the customer. Makes perfect sense, right?

If we're not careful, though, we can find ourselves behind the counter all the time. This is dangerous because we see the business from a place the customer never sees it. As a result, we make decisions that are logical to us but perhaps not logical to the customer.

It's why standing in front of the counter *during* lunchtime and not behind it can be challenging for a very busy business. At the same time, it's why seeing the business from the customer's perspective at the busiest time of the day is one of the most important strategies you and your team can implement.

What's the cure to insider-itis? *Seeing things from the customer's perspective.* When you see the business from the customer's perspective, the logical decisions we make from our perspective aren't so logical sometimes. Not responding to or engaging customers on social media seems logical to a big brand or organization. From a customer's perspective, it appears you don't care.

That may be unfair. It may be untrue. But it's their perception.

Perception is often what customers use to make decisions about a business.

And these perceptions are often ones a business can fail to see because it has unknowingly chosen producer logic over consumer logic.

Consumer Logic versus Producer Logic

Let me give you an example of producer logic in the quick-service restaurant industry. Producer logic says we need to get the food out as quickly as possible, which is true. As a result, there is a temptation to produce as many fries and food as possible and have it waiting in the chutes. That way, it's ready to go when the orders come in. This makes perfect sense from a producer's standpoint.

When you look at this with consumer logic, it's a really bad strategy if the quality of the food is jeopardized. The consumer doesn't care if *everyone* gets their food on time. They're interested in getting *their* food on time AND getting it hot and fresh.

There's nothing wrong with food in the chutes; there's something very wrong with food in the chutes if there's too much of it and the quality suffers.

Not only that, a ton of food in the chutes is something consumers see on the front side of the counter. They look at it and wonder, *How long has that been in there?* when you go to grab their sandwich or fries.

An example of this is movie popcorn. I'm a big fan of movie popcorn, especially the kind they sell at AMC Theatres. But I've learned a trick. Even though there may be popcorn in the chutes, I don't order popcorn. "Could I have a *fresh* bucket of popcorn, please?" It never fails that the employee behind the counter bypasses the popcorn in the chutes to go to the most recently popped popcorn. We both know where the freshest popcorn is, and ironically, it's not the one they are trying to sell. It may seem like a small thing to you, but don't forget—movie popcorn costs about as much as a down payment on a house nowadays. And since it feels that way, you want the best quality, right?

Granted, you could argue that the chutes help serve the consumer because it improves speed of service. Good point. The larger point, however, is to make sure you're basing that decision on consumer logic versus producer logic. When a consumer is ordering "fresh popcorn" over the popcorn in the chute, there may be a problem. The challenge is to make sure you are seeing your business from the front side of the counter. If not, we tend to see the business only from behind the counter. This is where stale popcorn lives and businesses go to die.

This is the danger of producer logic, and the scary part is that we are often victims of it and never know it. As a result, producer logic creates a very sinister disease called insider-itis.

An example of this can be found in the church, of which I'm a big fan. However, to a large extent, insider-itis is rampant here. I'm not suggesting we ignore insiders. I'm suggesting the gravitational pull is toward the insiders. I've received plenty of emails from insiders over the years. "Why is the music so loud?" "Why don't we start a motorcycle ministry?" Yes, I actually got that one. I have nothing against motorcycles. After all, I was a big Evel Knievel fan growing up. My point is that insiders will advocate for their position and interests. While that's fine and understandable, I don't think I've ever received a proactive email from an outsider saying something like, "Hey, I'd like to come to your church, but I was wondering . . ."

As a result, I have to be their advocate. I have to see the church from their perspective. Not only that, I have to see the church from the perspective of someone who is not on staff. For example, on Sundays I arrive at the church a couple of hours before our first worship gathering. At this time, there are no parking problems, no check-in lines, and all is wonderfully quiet. *I have perfectly created a system where I see no problems.*

It's why I love what Ed Catmull, the president of Pixar and Disney Animation, says about problems in his book *Creativity, Inc.* "What makes Pixar special is that we acknowledge we will always have problems, many of them hidden from our view; that we work hard to uncover these problems, even if doing so means making ourselves uncomfortable; and that, when we come across a problem, we marshal all of our energies to solve it."[6]

You shouldn't be discouraged if you find or notice a problem in your business. Nor should you discourage someone on the team when they bring up a problem, especially if they are seeing it from a consumer logic standpoint. You are seeing the business from their perspective. This is a huge win because it allows everyone to remember the main thing.

Part of the challenge is making sure everyone knows what the main thing really is. Most organizations assume clarity on this issue when that's not actually the case. But let's assume there is clarity. That's only half the battle.

Four Strategies for the Main Thing

Keeping the main thing the main thing is an antidote to insider-itis. You must proactively push against this malady. To do this, I want to provide you with four strategies that will help you lead your team in the fight against insider-itis and producer logic.

These four strategies will help you keep the main thing the main thing:

1. What you see
2. What you celebrate
3. Where you meet
4. What you talk about

1. What You See

Don't just say it. Show it.

Words are powerful, but research tells us over and over again that words *plus* images are more powerful. The walls of your organization should be dripping visually with vision. And yes, this can happen for virtual organizations as well.

One of the ways we push against insider-itis at Gwinnett Church is to repeat over and over again, "Every Sunday is someone's first Sunday." This isn't just a mantra. It's true. However, we can lull ourselves to sleep, thinking everyone knows where to park, where to go, and how long the service will be. We can talk as if they've been here from the very beginning. We will drift there if we aren't intentional and if we only rely on words.

It's why we created signs at strategic places for our Guest Services volunteers to see. We picked up this idea from the Notre Dame football team. On the way out to the stadium before the game, the players tap a sign that reads, "Play Like a Champion Today."

Our team does the same thing by tapping this sign—"Every Sunday Is Someone's First Sunday"—before they go out to serve. Visually showing the vision and creating a literal touchpoint is a powerful way to keep the main thing the main thing.

Gwinnett Church

Bottom line—keep the vision visible.

2. What You Celebrate

Another business hero of mine is Jimmy Collins, the former president of Chick-fil-A. Along with Truett, Jimmy helped build Chick-fil-A into what it is today. I learned so much from Jimmy, but one of the top lessons was "catch people doing right."

For many employees, they hear more from their boss about what's going wrong than what's going right. In fact, the first thing many employees think when the boss is calling is, *Oh no. What did I do?*

Sure, we don't need to shy away from correction and instruction. We also need to realize that celebration is a far better instructor. Jimmy was really good at correcting, but he was equally good at celebrating.

I remember one time walking into the bathroom and seeing Jimmy with a lighter, burning the edges of a document.

Typically, when a company president is burning documents, that's an alarming sign.

I realized that Jimmy was burning the edges of a sales report of a Chick-fil-A restaurant. He would scoop up the ashes and place them with the sales report along with a note to that particular operator. The note would read, "Wow! Your sales are on fire!"

Another classic Jimmy story: He'd walk back to the kitchen and ask, "Who made this pie?" He'd say it in a rather demanding tone. After a few moments of silence, someone in the kitchen timidly raised their hand, realizing perhaps that they had messed up in front of the boss. Jimmy walked over, put his hand on their shoulder, and announced to everyone in the kitchen, "This is an excellent pie. Exactly how it should be made!"

Do you think that employee remembered that day? Do you think it enhanced their passion for making the best pie possible, day in and day out?

This is the power of celebration. It helps reinforce the main thing.

It's why stories are so important. Sure, I believe in data. Data helps us make better decisions. But data alone rarely inspires. It's stories, celebration stories to be exact, that remind people of the main thing. (We'll talk more about this in section 2—FOR the Team.)

At Gwinnett Church, I asked our team to help me with this by finding stories to celebrate. They are able to see and hear stories collectively at a far greater rate than I can by myself. "If you'll find the stories, I'll find a way to share them" is what I've told our team. Here's an example of what I'm talking about.

Jenn Scholle worked in our environment called UpStreet

for elementary school students. Several Sundays in a row while working in UpStreet, she saw a little boy named Jack give money to the Giving Tree, which is a place where students can worship through giving. Jenn became curious and approached Jack's mom one Sunday and asked about it. She told Jenn that Jack does his chores at home and gets paid weekly. He brings in 10 percent of his income every Sunday for the Giving Tree. Jenn was so impressed that she asked me, "Is this a story you could share?"

"Jenn," I replied, "if I can't share this story, I need to find another line of work."

A few Sundays later, I told the church I wanted to highlight and thank one of our highest-percentage givers. I also said I wanted to give them an opportunity to thank this generous person who helps us move closer and closer to funding our potential. "It's generous percentage givers like this person who understand the power and joy of investing in the local church. Everyone, please join me in thanking Jack."

At this point Jack walked onto the stage. Here's a photo from that moment:

Gwinnett Church

Here's why I tell you this story. This moment would not have happened if it weren't for Jenn being on high alert for stories. She was partnering with me to celebrate a win—reminding everyone of what we celebrate at Gwinnett. We want to be known for being FOR Gwinnett. One of the ways we do that is to generously give of our time, talent, and resources. I believe a thriving, generous, caring church is one of the best gifts a community can receive. If we're not careful, we can drift toward insider-itis. When this happens, purpose leaves the building.

What does your organization celebrate? What are the stories you can tell? What is your system to find stories to celebrate? Remember, when purpose lives in an organization, an organization lives in purpose.

3. Where You Meet

There's nothing quite like seeing the business in real time, up close and personal. It's why I love having our leadership meetings in the community and not always at the church offices. The location reminds us of our purpose.

I could be wrong, but my guess is that most of your meetings happen at "the office." And with all due respect to Michael Scott, the office is fairly bland when it comes to real life. I'm not suggesting you shouldn't meet there. I am suggesting you shouldn't meet there all the time. Get outside of the four walls. It's where the best insights live. For those of you who work virtually, you can do the same. Don't always settle for a quiet home location. Get outside. Where you meet is a key strategy in the battle against insider-itis.

Rarely, if ever, have these words been said from a cubicle: "I have a breakthrough idea!" The reason is that cubicles shield us from the real world. Out there in the real world are problems—where great ideas go and hide, waiting for you to find them. It's what Greg Hale did in 1999 at Disney World. He began his career as an electrical engineer, but like any great team member, Greg had a passion for the company that went far beyond his job description.

As Greg walked around the park, he saw a problem. The success of Disney was creating more and more long lines, negatively impacting the guest experience. As he personally observed, listened to, and interacted with guests, the problem of long lines gave him an idea. What if guests could wait in line but not physically be in line? Thus the idea of FastPass was born.[7]

That's the good news. The challenging news is why did it take Disney from 1955 to 1999 to figure out a solution to the problem? Often it's because we aren't up close and personal enough with our guests to hear and see real-time problems.

It's why I believe one of the most important mantras to increase innovation and creativity is "get out of the office."

4. What You Talk About

Most meetings deal with the sustainability of the organization—sales, data, and projections, which are all very important and worthwhile. It's also why many organizations eventually fail. The sustainability of the organization unknowingly becomes the goal, and customers are a means to that end.

In your meetings, talk as much about the customer as you talk about the organization. Ask this question: "How is this helping the person we are trying to serve?" This will help you stay focused on the ones who will ultimately bring about your success—the customers.

Closing the Gap

The challenge with many organizations is how to close the gap between our two questions:

- What do you *want* to be known FOR?
- What *are* you known FOR?

Remember, customers tell customers where the gaps are between our marketing and their experience. Are we really FOR *them*? Or honestly, are we just trying to get them to be more FOR *us*?

It's why you need to show them real, authentic, and credible answers in order for them to become a sales force for free. And for this to happen, your organization must make a significant, simple, and systematic shift. If it's not at the heart of your business to do this, it won't happen.

But if the heart and soul are there, you will give your customers something positive to tell others. When this happens, it's priceless. When customers build a business, it is the healthiest form of growth there is.

This happens when you make a shift. It's no longer about convincing customers to become fans of your business. Your business has to stand for something more than that. The business isn't about generating fans.

It's about becoming one.

BECOME A FAN

Chubbies shorts.

The mere mention of this company and product often brings a smile. It's almost an oxymoron—two things that don't necessarily go together.

Like jumbo shrimp. Pretty ugly. And the Utah Jazz.

Chubbies is a brand with raving fans. Their sworn enemy is cargo shorts, and their motto is "life is too short for pants."

If you think this sounds like a company started by a bunch of frat boys, well, you'd be right.

But what they've done and how far they've come in such a short amount of time is a lesson for us all. If you like the idea of having a loyal legion of fans but achieving this at a very, very low cost, then you should keep reading. What they have done is smart, scrappy, and, here's the best news, fairly easy to replicate.

For quite a while now, businesses have been taught that the secret sauce to success is creating raving fans. The more raving fans you have, the more loyal customers you have. And while this makes perfect sense, what exactly is a raving fan?[8]

Here's one of my favorite definitions of a raving fan from

Chick-fil-A. A raving fan from their perspective is someone who does three things:

- pays full price
- visits more often
- tells others about the business

I like this. It's still relevant. It's still vital.

It's also changing.

The pathway to creating raving fans in a highly competitive, ever-changing business world isn't that easy. Yes, creating raving fans is important. How you get there is changing, and the quicker you get there, the better it will be, for you and your organization.

To help us get there, let me introduce you to the essence of the FOR strategy. I believe this is the pathway to future success for any organization that wants to thrive and grow:

> Winning organizations of tomorrow will be more concerned with becoming fans of their customers instead of convincing customers to become fans of the organization.

Adopting a FOR strategy is more than semantics. It is a call for a new way to view your business. Ultimately, customers aren't a means to an end. Instead, the business is a means to an end.

And while most organizations would argue they already

WINNING organizations of tomorrow will be more concerned with becoming fans of their customers instead of convincing customers to become fans of the organization.

know this, I'd counter by simply saying, "Knowing and doing are two different concepts."

In fact, it's rare—very rare—to see a company shifting the spotlight from the business to the customer. Customers are people, and people love to be seen, celebrated, and recognized. Often, a company is too busy talking about themselves instead of talking with the customer. Product shots and new deals too often get in the way of this.

It's why I love what Chubbies has done with their Instagram account.

To give you an example, let's compare Chubbies to Home Depot and Lowe's. Honestly, it's an unfair comparison in some ways to both sides. And yet, let's do it anyway. We'll learn something as we do.

As you know, our home improvement friends are both multibillion-dollar, ginormous enterprises. (And yes, *ginormous* is really a word.)

Chubbies, on the flip side, will hit annual revenues of more than $10 million. While $10 million is still a lot of money, in comparison to HD and Lowe's, it's, well, short. And yet, their traction on social media would lead you to believe Chubbies is the multibillion-dollar enterprise. Granted, you can't deposit Instagram likes and comments into the bank. However, I would be careful not to dismiss the connection between those two.

While Home Depot and Lowe's both have Instagram followers of more than 700,000 and 600,000, respectively, little Chubbies is coming in at more than 400,000. (This should cause you to raise an eyebrow.)

Furthermore, a typical post by Chubbies far outpaces the likes and comments that either Home Depot or Lowe's receives.

For example, as of today when I'm writing this, the most likes Home Depot received in the last month on an Instagram post was more than 8,800. The most likes Chubbies received in the last month on one post was more than 16,000—almost twice as many.

For Lowe's, I went back two months to find one that gained as much traction on Instagram. It hit 3,500 likes.

It's easy to dismiss this, and it's also easy to overexaggerate this. Both are problematic.

Instead, let's take the mind-set that there's something to learn from this. And again, I'm not trying to be unfair to Home Depot and Lowe's. I'm trying to be helpful.

So why does a men's shorts company have twice as much engagement on social media compared to these two giants of the home improvement industry?

Much of it has to do with where the spotlight is. Chubbies features their customers, while Home Depot and Lowe's feature products. Products don't engage on social media, people do.

Dismissing this example isn't a win. Leaning in and learning is.

Sure, you can be more nimble if you're a small company like Chubbies. But in some ways, that's my point, especially if you relate more to Chubbies than a multibillion-dollar enterprise.

The question we need to ask is, "How is Chubbies achieving this kind of social media traction on Instagram, while Home Depot and Lowe's are not?" Another question to ask, "How is Chubbies creating this kind of customer engagement that generates a loyal fan base?"

Simply put, in many ways, Chubbies has chosen to become a fan of their customers by spotlighting them on its Instagram feed. They have in essence turned over a large portion of their posts to their customers.

When you visit their Instagram page, you'll see lots of photos of customers. These are original posts from customers wearing Chubbies in which they tagged the company in hopes that they see it. When the team at Chubbies sees these posts, they often put them on the company's Instagram page—just like the customer was hoping they would.

It's a win-win for both. The customer is rewarded by seeing their post on the Chubbies Instagram page, and Chubbies is leveraging the credibility of a customer who's talking about their love for the brand. Again, it goes back to what Scott Cook said about the power and credibility of customers speaking positively to one another about your company. In this case, Chubbies is able to say, "See what our customers are saying about us." It's such a smart, inexpensive way to build an emotional connection with your customers.

WHEN you talk more about the customer than you do the business, the customer talks more about your business.

This is the power of being FOR the customer. When you talk more about the customer than you do the business, the customer talks more about your business.

Interestingly, one of the most popular recent posts Home Depot had was of a similar fashion. A post by customer @rxrodriguez7 featuring his son in an orange Home Depot apron was seen and posted by Home Depot, which generated a huge spike in Instagram engagement with more than 8,800 likes.

It's as if Home Depot thought they were Chubbies for a moment.

Sure, some people may not like a brand liking their social media posts, but when they are tagging the company, it means they secretly hope the company will. And you don't need me to tell you the research about what happens biologically when someone gets a photo liked on Instagram, Facebook, etc. It's powerful. And yet most brands never even go there to engage with their customers.

The larger point, however, isn't about social media.

The larger point is this: in order to create fans, you must become a fan.

This will require a proactive strategy we call "FOR the Customer." Very, very few brands are actually doing this. The spotlight is still shining brightly on the business.

That's great news for you because it means there's an opening here—you can proactively engage with customers in their world and on their terms, planting seeds that can yield a lifetime of results. And you don't need me to tell you the value of a lifelong customer. Great service alone no longer generates lifelong customers in and of itself. The power of lifelong loyalty happens when you surprise, wow, and engage them. It's why customer engagement is the new customer service.

Customer Engagement
IS THE NEW
Customer Service

CHAPTER 5

Most businesses forget the *social* in social media.

The reason for this is that social media is usually housed under the advertising department and is treated along the same lines as billboard advertising. There's nothing wrong with billboard advertising. It's just hard to have a conversation with a billboard.

Therein lies the power of social media—the potential to have a conversation with your customers in real time.

Granted, this is being done for the most part through customer call centers and to some extent Twitter. This, as you know, is customer service.

But again, the game is changing.

MOST businesses forget the *social* in social media.

If your business is going to truly be positioned to be FOR your customer, you must create systems to leverage the power of customer engagement.

Customer engagement is the new customer service.

What's the difference between the two?

Customer service is reactive; customer engagement is proactive.

Reactive customer service is:

Customer: "My fries were cold."
Company: "We are so sorry. Here's a coupon for your next visit."

There's nothing wrong with this. In fact, years ago, this kind of customer service would endear an organization to their customer. Today, it's expected. And if you don't deliver great service, word will spread. In fact, do you know where bad customer experiences go to live?

Yelp.

This is yet another reason I have such huge respect for today's business leaders. Every day requires you to bring your best. Customer service expectations haven't decreased. They have increased dramatically—primarily because great customer service is *expected*.

That's the challenging news.

Here's the great news:

- There is a new frontier in building a loyal customer base.
- This new frontier provides a unique competitive advantage.
- It's highly profitable with comparatively low expense.

It's a new frontier because very few organizations, if any, are actually living there now. Most organizations aren't thinking like this, which is why you need to act quickly. Who knows? Your competitors might be reading this book too.

The Land of Customer Engagement

Now before I explain it, let me challenge you to be open-minded about this phrase "customer engagement." For those of you in the nonprofit world, the word *customer* could be replaced with *member, volunteer, donor*, etc. For those in the start-up phase, simply think of these as potential customers. Proactively engaging with people online who are either customers or potential ones is where the game is going, at least if you want to let them know you are FOR them.

It's easy to see a phrase like this and think, *Oh, we engage with our customers.* And that's true. You do. However, few engage the way I'm about to describe.

The reason they don't is that it requires shifting the spotlight from the business to the customer. This, again, is the FOR way—to create or shift a business to be more FOR the customer than for the business.

The bad news is that it will require a change in thinking and systems.

The good news is that it's a low-cost, high-reward shift.

Excellent customer service is the foundation. Without it, you build your organization on shifting sand. But again, in today's world, it's just the beginning.

To move to the Land of Customer Engagement, you're going to have to break through an invisible barrier. I call it *invisible* because most, maybe all, organizations don't see it. As a result, they have no system for it.

As for you, you're about to be a step ahead. You are about to think differently. But don't just think differently; act differently.

And I'm about to show you how by leading you through the invisible barrier to the Land of Customer Engagement.

The Invisible Barrier

To give you an example of the invisible barrier, let's take our friends at Home Depot again.

As an Atlanta native, I'm a big fan of Home Depot. As a side note, my hometown has built more professional sports stadiums than we've won professional sports championships. This has nothing to do with what this book is about—I just want you to feel sorry for me.

At the same time, a cofounder of Home Depot, Arthur Blank, is the owner of the Atlanta Falcons. We were one quarter away from winning the Super Bowl. Again, I digress.

Let's take a look at Home Depot's Instagram page.

As of this writing, HD has more than 725,000 followers on Instagram.

Home Depot is currently following 421.

There's a lot I can say about this, but I'll keep it brief. Should Home Depot follow all of their 725,000 followers? Maybe. Maybe not. Should Home Depot follow more than 421? Absolutely.

The bigger point here is that it's a symptom of the spotlight being on the business versus the spotlight being on the customer.

Personally I like the look of Home Depot's Instagram page. It's sharp, engaging, and fun—just like print advertising should be. The problem is that it's social media—and there is no *social* happening. And as a fan of Home Depot, I want to quickly point out that most brands are in the same boat.

In fact, pick your favorite brand. Go to their Instagram page, and you'll see a gap between their followers and who they follow. Some will say they are concerned that a follow might imply an endorsement. You could always put a disclaimer in your bio that says a follow doesn't imply endorsement. Either way, large brands, and even small companies, would benefit greatly from becoming more personable on social media. And one of the ways to do that is to simply follow more of your followers.

That's one small step toward shifting the spotlight to shine more on the customer. But we're just getting started. The most impactful way to show your customer you are FOR them is to break through the invisible barrier.

The invisible barrier is when companies stay exclusively on their own social media platforms, never venturing onto the platforms of their customers. Home Depot, for example, has the potential of 725,000 possible customer engagement opportunities.

Let's take Dana, one of Home Depot's Instagram followers, who recently got engaged. A simple like of her engagement post and a comment—"Congratulations, Dana, from your friends at Home Depot"—would create a compelling, memorable moment for her.

It's a very personal way to engage with customers and to show them you are FOR them in the big moments in their lives.

It's also great for business. For example, fast-forward a year or so from now. It's a Saturday morning, and Dana and her new husband are working on their first home improvement project. As they drive down the road, Lowe's is on one side and Home Depot is on the other. Do you think the fact that Home Depot recognized them by commenting on her social media post might play into their deciding between Home Depot or Lowe's? Or what if Lowe's breaks through the invisible barrier before Home Depot does?

And while we're at it, to be fair, let's look at Lowe's. As of this writing, Lowe's has more than 664,000 Instagram followers. They are following 549.

That said, Lowe's is doing something that Home Depot isn't. We'll talk about that in the next chapter.

What neither is doing is breaking through the invisible barrier and engaging with customers on their platforms and in their lives.

Remember, customer service is *reactive*; customer engagement is *proactive*.

When we shift the spotlight from the business to the customer and have a "FOR the customer" mind-set, it changes the way we view our marketing and messaging.

Instead of shouting, "Look how great we are," thriving organizations will instead celebrate their customers and say, "Congratulations! You just got engaged."

Instead of saying, "Follow us on Facebook," thriving organizations will say, "We want to follow you on Facebook."

Instead of shouting, "Choose us," thriving organizations of the future will say to their customers, "We choose you."

Small and Scrappy

If you're reading this as a small-business owner, nonprofit leader, or church planter, it's easy to dismiss this and think, *I'm not a large brand or organization.*

But by dismissing this, you dismiss one of the greatest advantages you have! You can be small and scrappy. You don't have to turn a large ship in a different direction.

There's an old biblical principle that says, "Do not despise the days of humble beginnings." If you find yourself complaining about being a small organization in a world of larger ones, you are speaking your future into existence.

If you find yourself thinking of ways to leverage your advantage of being smaller in a world that is valuing personal interaction, you are also speaking your future into existence. For example, go to your Instagram page, click on the followers section, and break through the invisible barrier by visiting their Instagram page. Like a photo. Comment on it. Show them you're paying attention to them. Don't forget. They're already following you and interested in you. Returning the favor is small, scrappy, and smart.

It's why I love the story of Eryn Eddy and her clothing brand, So Worth Loving. The way she leveraged social media to put the spotlight of her company on the customer and community is a lesson for us all, for-profit or not, large or small.

Eryn didn't start out to create a clothing brand. Instead, she simply wanted to proactively engage with her growing fan base of music and YouTube videos. One of her videos went viral, and she wanted to do something proactively to thank her fans for their support.

"It meant so much to me that a community of people would share my music with their community of friends, and I wanted to do something to thank them. So I decided to create a T-shirt that wasn't about the music or me, but a message from my music that would encourage and uplift them.

"The phrase 'So Worth Loving' just came to mind. I stenciled and spray-painted a T-shirt with that message on it. Then I posted my home address online and asked my community to send me a T-shirt if they wanted me to spray-paint a shirt for them."

(Note: posting your home address online is probably an idea to avoid.)

"Yes, posting my home address was not a great idea! But again, I didn't think that many people would actually take the time to mail me a T-shirt. Well, I was wrong.

"I received over a hundred T-shirts in the mail! It took me a few months to fulfill all these requests. Along the way, I started hearing feedback from people who said they would prefer just to buy a shirt instead of mailing an old one.

"I started seeing a community being built when I received stories from people. When they began to hear the 'So Worth Loving' phrase, they started emailing me their stories about why they were struggling with self-worth. The common theme was they all felt alone. I had hundreds of emails from people who were saying they felt alone, but if they all knew each other, they wouldn't feel alone. They would feel like there is a light at the end of the tunnel, or maybe they would have the strength to seek help. I had an opportunity to show them they weren't alone."[9]

And that's when the idea of a company was born. Eryn quit her full-time job and decided to launch So Worth Loving on Black Friday in November 2011. But before there was an online sale, there was an online community. Too often, entrepreneurs can rush to market by building the product, but then they realize they haven't built a community. And that means there's no one to buy the product.

Before we can build a business, we must build a community.

Before the first T-shirt was sold, Eryn was already doing the foundational part of building a community through the stories she was receiving. "I emailed people back and asked if they would be willing for me to share their story on my blog. They could share their name or do it anonymously. When this started happening, more people would share their story on our blog. The courage to share their stories gave more people courage to share theirs. That's how we built this community, which feels like a family having a conversation.

"We aren't in the T-shirt or clothing business; we are in the self-worth business, which is communicated through apparel and clothing. Everyone in the So Worth Loving family knows this, and it's why we continue to proactively engage the people who are supporting this message."

Scaling Meaningful

What grew So Worth Loving wasn't the apparel, though the apparel is very important. What initially grew and sustains Eryn's company are the meaningful connections she has created with her community. She isn't treating her customers like an algorithm; she's treating them like people. I'm convinced more than ever that this kind of meaningful, personal, and individual connection is what will fuel growth in the future.

It goes back to the question Horst Schulze says customers are asking: "Do they really care about me?" It's why it's even more incumbent on large organizations to figure out ways to scale meaningful, personable interactions. It's why start-ups need to figure out how to do it from the very beginning. It's why churches, struggling to figure out the digital space, must leverage this new frontier in personable ways.

Intuitively, we know this works. We know what it feels like

as customers ourselves when an organization creates this kind of meaningful interaction. And yet when we get around conference tables and boardrooms, the skepticism can grow. *Does this really work? How do you know if this truly impacts the bottom line? How can we possibly create personal interactions with thousands and thousands of customers?*

It's why the research of the Havas Group is so important. Since 2008, they have been studying what impact, if any, brands receive when creating a meaningful connection between their customers. This research helps answer the age old marketing question, "How do we know if creating a meaningful, personal connection with our customers contributes to the bottom line?"[10]

Sure, it doesn't take away the question of whether specific marketing and advertising expenditures are worthwhile. Those factors still need to be explored. But the general theory of creating personal Wow moments with customers is often perceived as something you can't measure. And what you can't measure is often dismissed, to our detriment.

At the core of the FOR strategy is a theory suggesting that brands and organizations, churches included, need to stop talking about themselves so much. Instead, they need to start talking more about the customers and the community. Shift the focus from the business to the customer.

Granted, it was a theory until I read the research from the Havas Group. What they discovered is that when brands engage in meaningful, authentic, personable ways, customers respond. A "Meaningful Brand," the term Havas uses, is defined by its impact on our personal and collective well-being, plus its functional benefits. In other words, the question isn't, "Is this a good product?" The question is, "Does this brand care about us and me?"

It all seems a bit squishy and touchy-feely. Does this really work? Here are a few portions of the data.

First, why does being meaningful matter?

- People wouldn't care if 74 percent of the brands they use disappeared.
- Only 27 percent think the brands they use make life better. (In other words, they don't think most brands care.)
- 75 percent expect brands to make a contribution to our well-being and quality of life . . . yet only 40 percent believe brands are doing this.

Second, the question of whether or not meaningful, personal interactions impact the bottom line should be retired now. Between 2006 and 2016, meaningful brands have outperformed the stock market by a whopping 206 percent.[11]

THE more personable organizations can become, the more meaningful they will be.

Customers are savvy enough to know if we are focused on their well-being or simply focused on the well-being of the business. They can tell the difference and will reward the businesses that do. The more personable organizations become, the more meaningful they will be. Organizations that figure this out will win.

This is the new frontier. Customer service will get you there; customer engagement will keep you there.

Customer engagement proactively tells your customers something we all want to hear.

- "We see you."
- "We celebrate you."
- "We are here for you."

When done with authenticity and consistency, this creates meaningful interactions that customers share. And this is the wave of the future. Havas points out that 77 percent of millennials expect this kind of meaningful interaction from brands.[12] And indications are that the expectations of Generation Z will be even higher.

This is why structuring your organization around the FOR strategy is not just good business; it's vital for the long-term well-being of your organization to be concerned about the well-being of your customer and community.

DOING good is good for business.

And this is what is so exciting to me about this. Doing good is good for business. To not just talk a good game, but to truly show that you are FOR the customer and your community.

Choosing not to be afraid of being personable, vulnerable, and authentic.

Choosing to admit your mistakes when you make them.

Choosing to celebrate your customers and community.

Choosing to bet on purpose and meaning, even when you aren't sure it will flow to the bottom line. (Don't worry. It will.)

I know, I know. What about the dreaded word *how*? "How does this actually work?"

That's what the rest of the book is about. Creating a meaningful organization that impacts your customers, team, community, and you. All the while helping improve the world, one interaction at a time.

You see, purpose isn't exclusively reserved for nonprofits. When you foster a FOR culture in your organization, you create something bigger than the bottom line. You create purpose. You speak meaning. You get small and personal. And when you get small and personal, your customers will demand that you grow bigger.

Because, as you're about to see, small is the new big.

Small Is the **NEW BIG**

CHAPTER 6

One of the many lessons Truett Cathy taught me was the international sign if someone needs encouraging. This breaks through all cultural and geographical boundaries. Knowing this sign can help you in all areas of your life.

When you see this sign, it's your opportunity to encourage the person on the other side of you. From now on, you'll see these opportunities more clearly, not just in your business life, but in your personal life as well.

"The international sign to know if someone needs encouraging," Truett said, "is if they are breathing. If they're breathing, they need encouraging."

I'm a big believer in encouragement. I also believe I need to get better at leveraging the small daily moments of encouragement that are before me every day. Too often, I think we talk ourselves out of these moments. *Will it really matter? Will they really care?* And before you know it, the moment is lost. We talk ourselves out of encouraging someone because it just seems too small or insignificant.

But what if you created a culture that saw each day as an

opportunity to encourage your customers? What if no moment was "too small" in your company culture?

I think it would provide an unparalleled competitive advantage. Too many companies compete on price, while encouragement is priceless.

TOO many companies compete on price, while encouragement is priceless.

I'm convinced we need more CEOs—chief encouragement officers, and here's why: *encouragement is never small when you're on the receiving end of it.*

Everyone can recall a moment when a parent, coach, teacher, or friend spoke words of encouragement into us. One brief moment can stand the test of time. This is the power of encouragement, of noticing, of leveraging seemingly small moments into large memories.

Contrast this with a traditional advertising approach. Customers aren't seen as someone to encourage; customers are seen as someone who buys. This explains the Meaningful Brands research by the Havas Group. The reason 74 percent of customers don't care if brands disappear is because they don't think brands care about them.

While I don't profess to be an expert at your business, I do know something about each and every one of your customers. There are some good things and some challenging things going on in their lives right now. As the old adage says, "Be kind, for everyone you meet is fighting a hard battle." It's true for you. It's true for me. And it's true for every single one of your customers.

The thriving organizations of the future will truly and deeply care about their customers. They will think of ways to encourage customers, not just sell to them. And when this happens, customers will, in turn, care about you. This is the FOR mind-set.

Remember, our aim is to grow your business, church, or organization. But we grow in a counterintuitive way. We grow small.

Growing Small

As an organization grows, they can quickly lose the personal interactions with their customers that actually caused the growth. And it's easy to see why.

One day, you have a few customers. Then you have hundreds. Those personal touches that made such a big difference in the early days become few and far between. How can you possibly keep up? At some point, most business leaders give in to the reality of growing big. Before you know it, personal touches are replaced with efficiency. We scale the business by putting distance between human beings, and the heart of the organization is replaced with a machine.

Since we can't provide encouraging personal touches for everyone, we stop providing encouraging personal touches for anyone. Is it any wonder then why many large organizations drift off purpose? What got them there fades away.

Is this the plight of growing businesses and organizations?

We can learn how to do this from Dan Cathy, Truett's son and the CEO of Chick-fil-A. Dan grew up in the business, along with his brother Bubba and sister Trudy. They saw firsthand how their dad and mom knew customers by name and made the business personal. Dan saw how valuable those interactions were in building the business. He's passionate about maintaining those seemingly small moments that, in reality, aren't small at all to the customer. One of the ways Dan does this is by attending as many Chick-fil-A grand openings as possible. While it's not unusual for a CEO to attend a grand opening, what Dan does is highly unusual, personal, and memorable.

At every grand opening, the first one hundred customers are given coupons to eat free at Chick-fil-A for a year. That's right—a whole year. As a result, customers camp out in the parking lot in order to be one of the first hundred. Dan pitches a tent right alongside them and sleeps in the cold parking lot. While he could certainly be in a warm, nice hotel suite, the customers aren't there—they're sleeping in the parking lot. Thus, so is Dan.

The next morning, he rises early, gets out his trumpet, and plays reveille—welcoming them to a new morning, a new restaurant, and a new year full of free chicken.

I don't think you have to choose between corporate growth and personal touch. You simply must be intentional to create systems within the flow of every day. This is what it means to grow small.

It's why one of my favorite insights from Andy Stanley is this: *"Do for one what you wish you could do for everyone."*[13] This isn't just a great thought; it's a great system.

The opposite of this is what gets organizations into trouble. *"Since we can't do this for everyone, we can't do this for someone. Since we can't encourage and wow every customer, we won't encourage and wow any customer."*

When we're dealing with thousands, it's hard to see the one. But remember, the one is never just one. When we make a difference for one person, it spreads. That's the power of being

FOR someone. It's never stagnant. In one way or another, it spreads. They may tell others about your business or organization. It may just help them have a great day. It may help them in their story. When you do this, you become meaningful, personable, a difference maker.

Andy's insight takes the pressure off of trying to interact with *everyone* while maintaining the power of personal interactions by serving *someone*. This is a counterintuitive approach to growth because it scales the small memorable moments into the business.

Don't forget. One of the goals of this book is to help you harness the power of positive word-of-mouth advertising for your organization. For this to happen, you must give them something positive to say.

The more personable you are, the more remarkable you are.

And when people are remarking about your business, they have joined your sales force for free.

When a large, growing organization does something seemingly small for one customer, it's

THE more personable you are, the more remarkable you are.

not small at all to the customer. They begin to tell their circle of influence about it, and when this happens, it becomes bigger than just that one interaction.

You can fake great customer service with a television commercial; you can't fake great customer service in real life.

It's why these "small" moments aren't small at all. When we take time to encourage, or "do for one," it breathes life not just into the customer but into our organization. Because that moment is never small when you're on the receiving end of it.

Or what if you're just starting out? I know what you're thinking if you're an entrepreneur or church planter. *Jeff, I would love to have the problem of growing too big!* I get it. However, there are huge advantages to these early days. You have the opportunity to get this right from the very beginning and to scale these moments into your business. In other words, you have the opportunity to be a great friend to your customers. And as your business grows, so should that friendship. In fact, think of it this way . . .

Years ago, Wendy and I were celebrating our tenth wedding anniversary. To celebrate, we decided to take a short vacation to the Ritz-Carlton at Reynolds Lake Oconee. (In case you're counting, I'm up to two Ritz-Carlton examples.)

We checked in and were walking to our room, 511, when we noticed there was no room 511. There was a 509 and 513, but no 511. In the middle of the 509 and 513 was the presidential suite. That wasn't us!

"That's odd," I said. "The Ritz-Carlton doesn't usually make mistakes like this."

I mentioned to Wendy that I'd go back downstairs to let them know they gave us the wrong room when she pointed to the presidential suite and said, "See if the key works." My wife is the fun one in the marriage. Knowing the key wouldn't work, I decided to put the key in the door just for fun.

When I did, the green light came on.

I looked at Wendy and she said, "Shut up!"

I quickly put the key back in to see if it would work. Green light. Again!

This time, Wendy quickly opened up the door, and we

walked into our first-ever presidential suite. My memory of that moment is in slow motion, with rose petals falling from the sky and a symphony playing in the background. It was the largest hotel room I had ever seen.

There was only one problem. I knew we didn't belong. I turned to Wendy and said, "Maybe we just stay here until they figure it out!" At that point, we heard a knock on the door. *They had already figured it out.*

So I grabbed our bags and began the walk of shame to the door. Before I opened the door, I glanced through the peephole and noticed a Ritz-Carlton employee with a tray of chocolate strawberries. I love chocolate strawberries. It's healthy eating because, after all, strawberries are fruit.

I opened the door. "Mr. Henderson?"

"Yes."

"This is for you," he said. I slowly took the tray.

"Can we do anything else for you?" he asked.

Like, not kick us out? I thought. But instead I played it cool and said, "I think we're good." He said good-bye. I closed the door and turned around to Wendy. Once again she said, "Shut up!"

On the tray was a note. I opened the note, and then it all made sense. A few weeks before, I was having lunch with a friend of mine, Woody Faulk, and I mentioned to him that Wendy and I were about to celebrate our tenth wedding anniversary. He asked where. I told him and thought nothing of it.

The note said, "Wendy and Jeff, surprise! You've been upgraded! Welcome to the presidential suite. Happy tenth anniversary. Love, Woody and Rae."

That was twelve years ago. Kind gestures are wonderful for friendships.

Kind gestures are just as wonderful for business.

Can Woody and Rae do this for everyone? No. But it didn't stop them from doing it for someone. (And Wendy and I are so glad we were those someones!)

It's easy to dismiss this as a friend doing something nice for a friend. It's easy to think, *What does this have to do with my business?*

THRIVING businesses of the future will start seeing customers as friends.

It has everything to do with business.

Thriving businesses of the future will start seeing customers as friends.

The better a friend you are to your customers, the better a friend your customers will be to you.

This is why small is the new big.

Now, why am I making such a big deal out of this? It all goes back to becoming a fan of your customers. Think about it. What do fans do? They encourage and cheer on their team. When the team is down, they try to rally them. When a great play happens, they stand and cheer.

For far too long, a business has thought of itself as the one on the field while the customers are in the stands. This isn't the FOR way. Instead, the better mind-set is when the business thinks of itself as the fans in the stands cheering on the customers in the field.

To do this, to truly be FOR your customer, you're going to have to grow small by intentionally building this into your daily approach to the business.

It's why I'm so inspired by business leaders like Dana Spinola who are choosing to grow this way.

Dana is the founder and CEO of fab'rik, a growing women's boutique with forty locations. The vision of fab'rik is to "create boutiques where everyone can afford to feel beautiful, one piece of fabric at a time."

The core values of fab'rik are:

- Dream
- Hustle
- Inspire
- Wow
- Heart

There's so much to learn from Dana and her team, but let me point out how they systematize Wow. Like you and me, they inherently know it is no small thing when a customer is "Wowed." It has a ripple effect. But Dana doesn't leave this to good intentions. She has created a system.

"Delivering Wow is one of our key performance indicators," she said. "Each day, every one of our stores must report one Wow from the day. They send this along with their sales reports."[14]

Every day, when the franchise owners of fab'rik open their doors, they know one of their goals is to deliver at least one Wow to a customer. An example of a Wow was one Valentine's Day when a customer came in looking for something to wear for dinner that night. She mentioned to one of the staff members that she was concerned that they might not be able to go because they couldn't find a babysitter.

"I'll babysit for you," the staff member said. "You are such a loyal customer. It would be a great way for us to help you."

To which the customer said, "Wow!" Along with, "Here's our address. See you at 6:00 p.m."

You can't babysit *everyone's* kids; you can babysit *someone's* kids. Wowing one customer each day is a way to grow small. As Truett said, "We built Chick-fil-A one sandwich at a time."

We've applied this thinking to our Guest Services strategy at Gwinnett Church. Each Sunday, we serve around five thousand adults, children, and students. It's impossible for our volunteers and staff to create a personal interaction with everyone, but that shouldn't stop us from a personal interaction with someone. One of our Guest Services values is to deliver *Wow*—to serve our guests so well that they literally say, "Wow!"

To do that, we remind everyone that our goal every Sunday is for each of us to *Wow one person*. If each of us will commit to doing this individually, we will collectively Wow hundreds of our guests every Sunday.

It was easy to do this when our church was really small. It would also be easy to conclude that it's not possible to maintain this "small" feeling with thousands. I refuse to think that way. We can grow large. We can grow small. We can choose both.

This is a mantra to repeat to yourself and the team each and every day: *Personable leads to remarkable. Remarkable leads to memorable.*

The greater the WOW factor, the more memorable we become. Customers feel less like customers and more like friends.

They will remember how you made them feel, and they'll tell others about this memorable feeling.

The challenge is to not talk ourselves out of the small interactions our business or organization provides each and every day. In a very real way, this answers the HOW question from the previous chapter: *How do we create sustainable, meaningful interactions with customers?* Sure, there are lots of ways, but what if we just start simple, which is always the better way.

Let's WOW one person every day.

This humanizes the business. It keeps the heart and focus on where it should be—our customers. When we Wow a customer, we are reminded they aren't numbers.

They're people. And chances are they're breathing.

And as Truett said, if they're breathing, they need encouraging.

So encourage them. Wow them. Cheer them on. And when you do, something powerful happens.

They start cheering for you.

The Social **LOOP**

CHAPTER 7

My daughter Jesse is a big fan of the music duo Johnnyswim. A better description might be the word *obsessed*, as she likes to say. For Jesse's nineteenth birthday, Wendy and I bought concert tickets for her and our family. For an additional price, you could buy meet and greet tickets before the concert. When I saw the price for the meet and greet, I did what most dads probably do. I reminded everyone how much we're spending on college itself. Dave Ramsey would probably be proud, but I don't need to put the family on a guilt trip. Needless to say, we didn't buy the meet and greet tickets.

Then something happened. A WOW moment.

One Saturday, Jesse sends us a group text on our Fam Jam text thread that simply read "OH MY GOSH," along with a photo. The photo was an Instagram post of an organization she was interning with during the summer. The organization had a series of posts titled "Meet the Interns" that featured a photo of the intern with answers to two questions. Here's what the post about Jesse said:

- "One of her favorite smells? 'Brownies in the oven. There's nothing like it.'"
- "What song or artist has she listened to most often this past year? '@johnnyswim!!! I'm obsessed with them and am counting down the days until I get to see them in concert.'"

The post went on to say, "Now tell us your favorite smell in the comments! And then be sure to say hey to Jesse when you see her around camp this year!"

Guess who commented first?

That's right. @Johnnyswim.

"We love her already," they wrote. Followed by, "Fav smell: fresh honeysuckle."

I don't know how to describe what happened next in the Henderson family, other than to tell you that we later purchased four meet and greet tickets to go along with our Johnnyswim concert tickets. My apologies to Dave Ramsey.

Here's the point. That simple comment by Johnnyswim generated extra sales and a lifelong fan in Jesse's dad. Anybody who makes my daughter's day (year) like that is worth the extra support in my book.

It wasn't reserved for the Henderson family though. Jesse's friends were amazed by this, and it created quite the positive stir for a few days.

All this with One. Simple. Click.

This is why it's so important for organizations to leverage the *social* in social media. As we've been saying, social media is often treated as digital media—an electronic brochure. It's traditional advertising simply disguised in an online presence. As a result, this lack of engagement leaves dollars on the table. We fail to build the business by failing to build community.

Think of it this way. I have become a Johnnyswim advocate over that one simple comment. Not only have I told plenty of friends about it, but I'm now telling you! It's in this book, and who knows, maybe Johnnyswim is actually reading this right now. (If so, please help a dad stay cool, and comment on my Instagram page today.)

Johnnyswim shows us an important path for a business to follow: *the pathway to creating fans is becoming a fan.* In this case, Johnnyswim became a fan of Jesse's. And they added a few fans of their own in the Henderson family and others who have now heard this story.

Checking the Other Box

When people are asked how they heard about a company or product, there's usually a list of choices:

- television
- radio
- billboard
- direct mail
- other

Other always gets the most votes. We all know who *other* is. It's a friend, a neighbor, a coworker, who said those priceless words, "Hey, have you ever tried . . ." and they filled in the blank with your organization's name. We all know word-of-mouth advertising is the greatest form of advertising there is. It's why I'm puzzled that so many organizations, large and small, don't work toward leveraging the social in social media to create this. Again, this isn't as much about social media as it is about creating a business that engages with customers on their turf. Social media simply provides a fast, efficient way for this to happen.

Just for fun, I'll occasionally comment on a company's Instagram page. I guess you could say it's a hobby of mine, which I know sounds like a lame hobby. "Why not take up golf?" you may ask.

Well, I did that once. It wasn't great for my spiritual life.

So I'll save money on the greens fees and comment on the Instagram pages of some of my favorite organizations. It's all part of a test. I'm just curious how long it takes to get a response back. If ever.

I rarely do.

As I've been alluding to in the previous chapters, this is more than just a small miss on social media. It's an indication of a systems problem. More problematic, it's a sign that there needs to be a strategy shift. At the center and focus of the business strategy is the business. Our decisions, our strategies, our meetings are all designed to prosper the organization. It all makes perfect sense . . . to the business. Therein lies the problem.

Nowhere is this more evident than in the general approach to social media. The invention of social media should be a gift to every business and nonprofit organization. What happens is a different story. We put it through the "FOR the business" filter and simply turn social media into digital advertising. There's nothing wrong with that, but we need to stop calling it social media. It's just media. There is no *social*.

As a result, it becomes an extension of our advertising that never fully harnesses the power of what could be. For example, I'm convinced that I'm probably harnessing 10 percent of the capabilities of my iPhone. There's so much more I can do with it that I just haven't gotten around to discovering. The same is true when it comes to being FOR the customer. It's why I want to provide a different approach to social media. It's less about us and more about the customer. It's the way it should be.

To fully harness the power of social media, organizations must consistently walk on what I call the *social loop*. Whenever an organization posts something, the loop begins. Customers and followers may start responding, and a conversation loop has begun. Here's how it normally works:

- The organization posts.
- A follower responds.
- The organization does nothing.

Well, at least nothing from the organization's side. The

followers start talking to one another, but the organization has stopped engaging on this post because they're working on the next post. As a result, the conversation loop is rarely, if ever, closed.

Here's the ironic part. The better the post, the more comments that post will generate. The better your organization becomes at developing engaging and interesting content, the more the social loop with customers goes unclosed.

Think of it this way. You're having coffee with a friend. You start the conversation. They respond. You say nothing. Or worse yet, you get up and leave and go to another table. How would that make your friend feel?

This is exactly how a customer feels when they comment on a post and a business doesn't respond. I've shared this with small and large organizations. Everyone usually agrees, but then they respond with a systems question: "But how do we do this with limited staff? We're just trying to be consistent with content, much less respond to the comments."

It's a great question. It's why I want to provide you with a system that helps you engage consistently on the social loop. I'm going to list four common mistakes to avoid and then four principles to organize around. I want you to begin using this as your filter as you see other organizations implementing social media. You'll never see social media the same again. And that's a good thing—FOR your customers and your business.

Again, this isn't as much about social media as about leveraging social media as a way to cheer on your customer. This is an incredible platform that, when used correctly, shifts the focus from the business to the customer.

Four Social Media Mistakes You Can Easily Avoid

Mistake #1: Treating Social Media as a Megaphone and not a Telephone

A megaphone approach highlights the business where the primary emphasis is promotion. Instead, think of social media as a telephone—an opportunity to have a conversation with your customers. Sure, that doesn't mean you don't post about products or services. But all of that is secondary to creating a real connection with your customers, one in which they feel noticed and appreciated.

Mistake #2: Believing That Content Management > Customer Engagement

In most organizations the emphasis is on posting about the organization and then moving on. This shows the organization is more interested in "looking good" than in being personal and engaging with their customers.

If you work for a large organization, this can be a frustrating comment. For example, in one of Coca-Cola's Instagram posts, they received more than a thousand comments. How could they possibly respond to every one of those comments? Great question.

The point isn't to try to comment or respond to everything. The point is to create a game plan to comment and interact more. And, as I've studied Coke's Instagram feed, they are doing that, occasionally. My hunch is that Coke doesn't have a system for this. Most organizations don't. Sure, they have a social media department perhaps, but the approach rarely provides interaction.

Here's why this is important. For companies to truly leverage social media, they are going to have to up their game with personal interaction. *The more personable the interaction is, the more remarkable the experience will be.* And customers will notice. To use the old but still true analogy from hockey star Wayne Gretzky, "I don't skate to where the puck is. I skate to where the puck is going."

When it comes to social media, personal engagement is where the puck is going. The companies and organizations that figure this out and systematize engagement are the ones who will increase loyalty. Most organizations outsource their content management. Why not do the same with customer engagement?

That said, here's today's homework. Visit your organization's Instagram, Twitter, or Facebook page and give yourself a grade on the responsiveness and interaction you are having. Then for fun, comment on one of your favorite organization's social media platforms. Let me know when you get a response back.

Mistake #3: Valuing Social Media over Email

It's common nowadays for organizations to have a social media strategy, but it's rare for an organization to have a proactive and effective email strategy.

There's often a perception that email is a hated necessity of life. The reason for this isn't because of email. It's because email isn't leveraged in the right way.

The other reason we should value email is because Facebook can't change the algorithms on our email list. Your email list is of greater value than your social media followers because you have more control over what gets seen. That said, it's not enough to simply send emails. We must have a content strategy.

Here's a great exercise for you and your team. Find the last email your organization sent and read it. Did it add value or just provide information? The answer dictates the open rate of emails.

This is especially true for nonprofit organizations. Chances are you have a fairly sizable email list based on who participates in your organization. The typical email approach is to send out information about an event, how to contribute financially, or the latest news about the organization. This is why the open rates to emails are often so low. The subject line isn't intriguing, and the content usually is asking something of the reader.

Admittedly, we need customers to buy or donors to donate. It's not that we should be unclear about a call to action. We simply need to use a better approach.

For example, nonprofits generate a large percentage of their annual revenue in December. This results in a barrage of emails the last week of December. What many nonprofit organizations may not realize is that *every other nonprofit* is doing the same thing. As a result, these emails are now competing with one another.

A few years ago at Gwinnett Church, we decided to try a different approach. We started earlier in December and actually sent more emails, not less. This is counterintuitive because it's assumed the more emails an organization sends, the more unsubscribes it will receive. It all depends on the value of the email.

We started sending emails that featured, for example, a Spotify Christmas playlist. The next email included a college football bowl schedule while the next one included a Christmas breakfast recipe. Each one included a year-end giving button. The open rates of these emails were 30 percent while the standard for open rates is generally 24 percent.

The strategy was to increase the open rate of our emails by

increasing the value of our emails. By adding value, it increased not only the open rate but also helped spur year-end giving to the church. This also allowed us to send more emails than usual. The first year we did this, I was very apprehensive because I was concerned we would receive many unsubscribes and create a negative backlash. The exact opposite happened. We actually had people inquiring how to sign up for our email list because they had heard about it from friends.

It goes back to having a FOR mind-set for your audience. Rather than sending one email asking for money at the end of the year, begin with asking how you can add value to your email audience.

Mistake #4: Never Visiting Customers' Social Media Platforms and Interacting with Them There

If we were in a room together, this is where I'd stand up to illustrate this point. I would walk around, using phrases such as "game changer," "FOR the customer," and "remarkable leads to memorable," and I'd end big with, "It's not about us. It's about them!"

I mentioned the invisible barrier in chapter FOR—you know, the one before chapter 5. ☺ The problem with never breaking through the invisible barrier and staying on your own platform all the time is you never realize what could have been. For example, Johnnyswim would have never received additional sales if they had just remained on their own platform. Instead, they ventured onto the platform of High School Summer Camp, and the rest, as the Hendersons say, is history.

I have no idea how to calculate the potential earnings of organizations if they began to systematize around customer engagement like this. Instead, we spend way too much time on photo shoots and social media promotions instead of becoming more personable with our customers. I'm not suggesting organizations shouldn't do photo shoots and social media promotions as ways to create engagement. This activity actually generates the potential that is so often left untapped by many organizations.

Granted, this is somewhat easier for smaller organizations due to a smaller number of customers. However, when an organization comments on a customer's Instagram page, for example, it is creating a bond, which is both remarkable and buzzworthy. It almost guarantees the customer will be honored and will tell their friends. Therein lie the potential and power of word-of-mouth advertising.

With this in mind, here are four questions for you and your team:

- When's the last time your organization liked an Instagram post, a Facebook post, or a tweet from one of your followers?
- When's the last time your organization commented on a customer's social media platform?
- What is an example of your organization reaching beyond its social media platform and engaging with a customer?
- What systems do you have in place to ensure that your organization interacts with customers on their social media platforms?

All of this leads us to the "FOR Your Customer" strategy.

What we want to do here is create a strategy where we proactively engage with customers in their world and on their platforms. The goal is to show them that we truly *are* FOR them. We aren't some unfeeling, monolithic brand. We're real. We're here. We're cheering them on.

Four Strategies FOR Your Customer

Strategy #1: Follow Your Followers

First things first. Your organization needs to follow more people than it is currently following. It's amazing to me the follower discrepancy, especially when it comes to large brands. I don't understand the pushback as to why brands or organizations wouldn't want to follow everyone, or at least a lot more than they currently are. One excuse I've heard is that by following someone you don't know, you somehow agree with everything they post. Well, there's always the unfollow button.

Let's not forget that it's called *social* media for a reason. Along those lines, instead of asking customers to "follow us on Twitter," we should let them know we want to follow them. It's normal for businesses to ask customers to follow them on social media. Don't be normal. It's a better, more personable approach to say, "We want to follow *you*."

This shifts the spotlight from the business to the customer.

If this isn't something your organization is quite ready for, then try this. Search your company's name with a hashtag. Let's try this out as an example. Let's pick Fisher-Price, a company that produces educational toys for children. #FisherPrice currently has more than 504,000 posts on Instagram—and as far as I can tell, not a single one has been liked by the company. (I must confess I haven't checked every single post of the 504,000, but every post I did check wasn't liked by Fisher-Price.) If you want to be more remarkable by being more personal, you must start leveraging these posts. How?

Well, that's what the remaining three strategies are for.

Strategy #2: More Dialogue, Less Monologue

I recently visited Panera Bread's Instagram account. They posted a photo of a customer's post, which was a good idea, much like Chubbies does. Again, this strategy may not be for everyone, but it generated a lot more likes than usual for them—which leads me to believe it does work.

Additionally, they received fifty comments—not a single one was liked or commented on by Panera. This is a monologue approach that, in essence, ignores the customers.

I believe if you aren't going to dialogue with customers on social media, you should probably just stop posting. When a customer speaks and you don't dialogue, it's rude. It's better just to be quiet on social media than to stir up comments that are left in cyberspace for the rest of us to see.

However, there's a better way. *More dialogue.* Create a system where you can leverage the feedback and customer interaction your social media is creating. If not, you end up marketing to your own detriment.

Strategy #3: More Likes, Fewer Posts

The emphasis here is to talk more about your customers and less about you. A specific way to do that is to break through the invisible barrier and engage with your customers by liking their posts. Very few, if any, brands do this, which is why it's an opening for you. Your competitors aren't there. Your competitors are too busy talking about themselves, while you can be focused on talking with your customers. It's personable, which makes it both memorable and remarkable to your customers.

Here's an example of how it can work. Let's start with the people who follow your organization on Instagram. Simply click on their page and then on a post, and like it. You can comment on it as well. But the comment isn't about you. It's certainly not "check out our latest offer." That's about *you*. That's not what we're going for.

Your new strategy is to like customers' posts more than you post yourself. A goal would be fifty customer engagements each day. This may seem like a small thing, but it's not when you're on the receiving end.

At Gwinnett Church, we begin our staff meetings by going to Instagram and searching the hashtag #ForGwinnett. Our goal is for each of us to like ten posts and comment on two.

Remember, the more personable, the more remarkable. You get personal with customers when you comment or like what they're posting. And don't fall prey to the thinking, *But I can't comment or like everyone's post.* Remember what Andy Stanley said: "Do for one what you wish you could do for everyone."

What we need here isn't an excuse; what we need is a system.

Yesterday a friend of mine was telling me how much his daughter loves American Girl dolls. My daughter loved them too when she was growing up. As I was writing this chapter, I decided to visit their Instagram page and see what their approach was. (See, I told you it was a hobby of mine.)

At the time I'm writing this, they have 387,000 followers and are following 300. We've already commented on this, so I'll move on. What I've observed is they do a good job of responding to the first four or five comments, and then they go quiet. My hunch is they don't have a system to consistently engage with customers on social media, at least not on Instagram, as far as I can tell.

A few weeks ago, I was meeting with the chief marketing officer of a multibillion-dollar brand, showing him the content of this book and specifically the "FOR your customer" idea. "I get it, Jeff," he said, "but the problem is we're already swamped, and I can't hire another fifteen people to do this."

Exactly.

But we can't let this truth be the final word. I believe there are ways to outsource this work while at the same time being true to the personality of your brand and creating a personal human touch online. For example, I can remember when there was a day that companies didn't have social media departments. We've since figured that out. We can figure this out as well. If you don't, your competitors just might.

Either way, your organization needs to create a customer engagement system where you are proactively engaging with customers where they are and about what's happening in their lives. As you do, you'll show them you are a fan of theirs, are really FOR them, and are paying attention to what's happening in their lives.

Strategy #4: Talk More about the Customer, Less about the Business

At this point, I think it would be helpful to do a communications and messaging inventory. Look at your last ten social media posts and determine where the spotlight is. Is it on your customers and larger community, or is it on the business? The goal isn't to stop talking about the business or organization; the goal is to achieve a better balance in order to be consistent with the purpose of the organization. Too often, the messaging implies that the goal is to "keep the business alive." While that's important, it's not the purpose of thriving organizations. It's not how you close the gap between the two questions.

One of the ways we attempt to find this messaging balance at Gwinnett Church is by posting about the community every other post. We don't always get this right, but it's a goal. We want to be known for being FOR Gwinnett County, but if all we're doing is talking about Gwinnett Church, it rings hollow. An example of how we do this is by featuring local businesses in the community. It's impossible to have a thriving community without thriving businesses. Supporting and cheering them on are ways to show we're FOR Gwinnett.

Gwinnett Church

An example is this post on the Gwinnett Church Instagram page about Karissa Norfleet, the owner of Simply Done Donuts:

Hey #Gwinnett—next time you are in downtown Duluth, stop by Simply Done Donuts! Owner Karissa Norfleet started this business three years ago with just a donut truck. Karissa loved this experience because it allowed the business the freedom to provide donuts to different markets before deciding where to set up shop. "Duluth was #1 on our list and then out of the blue, after an event, we saw a sign up for the new development that is Parson's Alley and jumped on it." The shop opened in March 2017 and has been thriving since, providing bite-size donuts and delicious coffee to the community of Duluth. @simplydonedonuts prides themselves on their relationship with their customers. "We take the time to talk to you and listen," Karissa said. "We build a bond, friendships, relationships, that help continue to grow the community that is Duluth." Karissa is so thankful that Gwinnett has provided the perfect home for Simply Done Donuts. Are you searching for a part-time job? Well, you're in luck. Simply Done is searching for help in the mornings. Contact them for more information. #ForGwinnett

What would this look like for you? How can you shift the spotlight from the business and start highlighting the people in and around your business?

This is where thriving businesses are moving to—less *transactional* and more *relational*.

The Value of a Lifelong Customer

When you focus on the relational over the transactional, more transactions happen because you've earned a customer for life. And we all know the lifelong value of a customer isn't just the business they provide, but the business they help bring in by telling others about us. It's not just about acquiring customers. The true value is in *keeping* customers. But the pathway to getting there is changing. You must show your customers the heart you have for them—consistently. You must be more personable, more engaging, and more focused on them and FOR them. To help with this, check out the link in the bonus section to "Social Media Made Simple."

If all this sounds a little touchy-feely, well, welcome to the new frontier. To be FOR your customer, we're going to have to become a lot less corporate and a lot more personable. To reap the benefits of lifelong customers, we're going to have to give them a reason to continue to choose us. To create a sales force for free, we're going to have to give them something to talk about. This rarely happens with price and promotion. It rarely happens with sleek advertising. It's less about price. It's far less about promotion. It's all about purpose.

And that purpose is no longer about us.

It's all about them.

It's all FOR them.

In turn, it's how they become FOR us.

SECTION 2

FOR THE TEAM

CHAPTER 8

IN FAVOR OF

My favorite definition of the word *FOR* is "to be in favor of."
Imagine a world where team members are in favor of
one another.

Imagine a world where churches are in favor of one another.

Imagine a world where employers are in favor of employees,
and vice versa.

It sounds so simple. It's also so very rare.

I love this concept of "to be in favor of." It doesn't mean you
lower the standards. Far from it.

When you are in favor of, your standards rise.

When you are in favor of, you believe more.

When you are in favor of, you are others-focused.

Who wouldn't want to work in such a place like that? And
with people like this?

It's what this section is all about—to be in favor of the team,
to be FOR the team.

One of the best ways to live out your purpose and be
FOR your customer is to be FOR your team. It's impossible to

consistently be in favor of your customer when you're consistently at odds with the team.

Here's why: *how the team is treated is eventually how the customer is treated.*

For example, when I walk into a business, I can tell within thirty seconds how the team is being treated because it flows to me, the customer. When the business is FOR the person behind the counter, I can see it on their face. I can hear it in our conversation. I feel it in how I'm being treated. And I'm not the only one. Every single customer experiences the team culture of the organization because, good or bad, what happens behind the counter flows to those of us in front of it.

An example of this is what I experience every time I walk into Sid Mashburn's store. GQ magazine named Sid's business the "Best Men's Clothing Store in America." That's high praise for a shop that opened with one location in 2007, competing against massive clothing stores that have been around for decades. Not only that, Sid opened his store in the worst financial recession since the Great Depression. Despite this and other challenges, customers became a sales force for Sid, spreading the word about him. It eventually flowed all the way to GQ and now to you.

What's Sid's secret?

Sure, he has outstanding products. But so do a lot of his competitors. One of Sid's distinguishing characteristics is customer service. But behind the service is how he serves his team. Or, rather, family.

"When you spend eight hours a day, five days a week with people, I think they become more than a team. It's somewhere between team and family. That's how I see it. We celebrate together. We agonize together. We holler at one another. We encourage each other. It's just like a family.

"So when my wife, Ann, and I had been working on this business, we wrote down what we wanted to be known for . . . other than clothes. She has a shop next to mine—Ann Mashburn—and we both knew it wasn't enough to just offer great stuff.

"The first two words that came to mind were *hopefulness* and *helpfulness*," Sid said. "If our team doesn't experience hopefulness and helpfulness working here, our customers will never experience it shopping here.

"It's very important that the people who work here realize their role isn't just selling clothes; their role is taking care of people.

"Another question we ask ourselves is, 'How do we enhance someone's life?' We believe hopefulness and helpfulness is the way.

"This isn't a business philosophy; it's a life philosophy."[15]

Let's apply our two big questions to the Sid Mashburn work culture by asking them this way:

- When it comes to the team, what does Sid Mashburn want to be known FOR?
- When it comes to the team, what *is* Sid Mashburn known FOR?

The goal of Sid and his team is to make sure the answers "hopefulness and helpfulness" are the same to both questions. When they are, hopefulness and helpfulness flow from the team to the customers, enhancing lives.

Again, this is where corporate purpose lives. Sure, every organization has some sort of statement about valuing their employees. The thriving ones actually live up to it. Healthy organizations don't just talk a good game; they walk it. Ensuring that these two questions match is a pathway for that journey.

Lessons for the Journey

As I look back over my career, I have been blessed to work for some amazing organizations and people. I've worked with too many incredible people not to reflect on, capture, and pass along the lessons I've learned. What I've noticed is most of the moments and lessons I remember are simple—so simple that they are often overlooked in how we teach business today. They are often hidden beneath the rubble and onslaught of data and spreadsheets.

Being human still wins in business. Going out of your way is often better than pointing the way. Even in today's high-tech, fast-paced world, people still are drawn to humility when it is displayed in the workplace. The same is true with kindness. Kindness and humility are great for business. So are hopefulness and helpfulness. Either way, it's often the soft skills that make all the difference in the workplace and our careers.

We all know very talented, smart people who lack emotional intelligence. They have the hard skills but not the soft skills. As a result, there is a lid on their potential. This isn't just true for individuals, however. It's true for organizations as well.

There are plenty of talented, well-resourced teams. For many, their culture lacks the vital, soft skills to move them forward. Soft skills aren't soft at all. Ultimately, it's what defines your culture. It's what happens when you create a FOR culture, one in which you are in favor of both the team and the customer.

In this section, I want to share practical examples of how to do this and package it in a way that each of us can emulate. Sure, you'll do this in your own style, but I believe this can be a guiding path toward creating a culture that flows from the team to your customer in ways that grow the business and people.

It's not just important.

It's everything.

As Peter Drucker reportedly said, "Culture eats strategy for breakfast."[16]

That said, here's what's on the menu.

CHAPTER 9

Designing a
FOR CULTURE

Your culture is created by default or by design.

There is no middle ground. We're either moving forward or backward.

A team culture that's in decline will be hard-pressed to create a sales force for free—positive word-of-mouth advertising. Remember, how the team is treated is eventually how the customer is treated.

Knowing this, I want to give you a pathway based on my observations and experiences working for thriving organizations, as well as being around incredible leaders I've had the opportunity to meet. This, I believe, will help you design a FOR culture for the team. It's a simple, five-step, continuous process that elevates the soft skills and emotional intelligence of any group. Here's what it looks like:

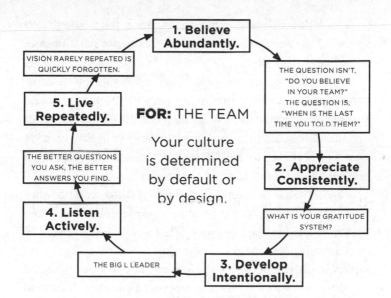

Obviously, this isn't an exhaustive list. And yet these soft skills provide an energy, a feeling, a passion, that hard data in and of itself just can't.

- Believe abundantly.
- Appreciate consistently.
- Develop intentionally.
- Listen actively.
- Live repeatedly.

By following this pattern, I believe you can create a team culture that will eventually flow well beyond the borders of the office.

Think of it this way. What do you think you would hear if you asked the people you worked with this question: What does it *feel* like to work here?

It's an important question because feelings often drive behaviors. It's certainly true in our personal lives, but it's also true in our corporate lives. What do you think the impact on an organization would be if the consistent answer to this question was, "I feel believed in. I feel deeply appreciated. I feel developed and challenged. I feel heard. Consistently."

Not only that, what if it flowed to the customer when they were asked, "What does it feel like to do business here?" and they responded in the same way. What would the difference be in nonprofit organizations if this kind of feeling and emotion welled up in the hearts of those who are participants in the mission? This isn't some nice strategy to implement. It's a vital strategy, at least if we want to engage the hands of people in the work before us. You won't engage the hands of people without first engaging the hearts of people.

It's not easy, but neither is it complicated. All of us can design a FOR culture where we grow the people with whom we work and do business. And while there are lots of ways to get there, designing a FOR culture is a vital pathway to follow.

WHERE
Innovation Lives . . .
OR DIES

CHAPTER 10

"**I** believe in you."

I was a recent college graduate starting my first full-time marketing job. Not only that, it was my first meeting of my very first day.

I was sitting across the street from the State Capitol in Atlanta meeting with my boss Steve Polk. Mr. Polk was a long-time executive with the state of Georgia, and he had given me an opportunity to do marketing work for Georgia tourism. I was as green as the Boston Celtics, but for some reason, he saw potential in me.

Little did I know it at the time, but Steve Polk would end up becoming not only my first business mentor but a lifelong influence on me. Part of the reason was the four words he used to start our meeting.

"I believe in you."

Looking back, there probably weren't a lot of reasons to truly believe in me. Honestly, *I* had my doubts about me. But his belief triggered something in me. He saw something in me that I didn't see in myself. And I wanted to prove him right.

This is the power of *believing abundantly* about people on the team. Belief causes people to rise to the expectations.

Here's why: *people who are believed in work harder than those who aren't.*

Growing up, I was very involved in sports. During this time, it was often the coaching strategy to yell, criticize, demean, and doubt players. The strategy was that by doing this, the coach would create a desire for the player to prove the coach wrong. "We'll show you that your lack of belief in us is wrong" was the mind-set coaches wanted to instill. And it worked for some teams.

It was also highly manipulative, with a short time frame. Most coaches coach specific players for a very limited time. Once the eligibility of the player is done, a new group appears. A new group to doubt. Over time, though, this approach wears thin. People leave. It may work at four-year schools, but at work, people just leave. And not only is a high turnover rate financially costly; it burns the culture at an even faster rate.

It doesn't mean you don't challenge. It doesn't mean you don't confront. The exact opposite happens. Belief allows you the platform to call everyone to a higher standard.

My friend David Farmer is the vice president of restaurant experience at Chick-fil-A. He is known for having very candid conversations with his team. "I believe in you, and I believe I can help you move even closer to your potential," he'll tell each team member. "To do that, we're going to have some honest, candid conversations from time to time. But all of this is based on my belief in you and in what you can do."

My experience is that team members want this kind of feedback. The most harmful feedback isn't negative; the most harmful feedback is none at all.

Belief is instilled by design, not by default.

Therefore the question isn't, "Do you believe in your team?" The question is, "When is the last time you've told them?"

Believing abundantly allows you to fight off one of the greatest dangers within any organization: *fear*. Thriving organizations deeply desire to have a spirit of innovation. Without it, the pace of change outside the organization will quickly outpace the change inside the organization. When this happens, the end is near.

However, we have to understand a truth about innovation and organizations.

Organizations don't stop innovating. People do.

The reason people stop innovating is because of fear. They are afraid of failing. The problem with this is you can't have innovation without mistakes. Just ask Thomas Edison.

ORGANIZATIONS don't stop innovating. People do.

Innovation is fueled more by belief in the team than criticism of the team.

Belief sparks innovation. Criticism sparks fear.

The question then is how do you balance belief and challenge?

Author Dr. Tim Irwin makes a great distinction in his book *Extraordinary Influence*. "One of the phrases that we've heard all of our lives is *constructive criticism*," Dr. Irwin writes. "What it usually means is that I'm going to gut you emotionally, but my motives are positive."[17]

Dr. Irwin is on a personal crusade to eradicate the term *constructive criticism* from corporate life. Seriously. He has a petition you can sign at www.drtimirwin.com.

Obviously, this leads to an important question: If we can't criticize someone and tell them what's wrong, how can that person improve and get better?

It all goes back to being FOR the other person. "I strongly believe that if we know deep down a person is *for us*, we can hear just about anything they convey to us," Dr. Irwin says.[18] "If we want to bring out the best in another person, we are more likely to do so if we form an alliance intended to help the person."[19]

Dr. Irwin describes a different approach, which he calls "Alliance Feedback."[20]

Constructive criticism is top down. "You are not meeting *my* expectations." Alliance Feedback is peer-to-peer. "You are not meeting *your* expectations."

See the difference? In this case, we take the time to get to know the person and their aspirations, hopes, and personal standards. We create an alliance with the people we lead and serve.

Alliance Feedback is where a manager aligns herself with the employee, helping them live out who they truly want to become. When the personal and corporate standards aren't being met, the manager reminds them of their own personal expectations.

Great managers and leaders understand they don't have to choose between what's best for the organization and what's best for people. Far too often, what's best is what's best *for both*.

It's why the four words Mr. Polk spoke over me all those years ago are still with me today. Eighteen months after that first day, he was diagnosed with an aggressive form of cancer. Steve Polk passed away on my birthday, March 7. Every year on my birthday, I'll either drive out to his gravesite or pause to reflect on how I am living up to the belief he abundantly spoke over me.

He was the kind of leader I want to be.

He was the kind of person I want to be.

Work provides an opportunity for me to try to live this out for others.

It's why believing in people isn't just a great way to do business; it's a great way to do life.

How to Create
A POSITIVE
Team Culture

One of the observations I've made about thriving organizations is they have a culture of deep appreciation. There is a genuine and active gratitude for the team and the work everyone does. The word *active* is important. Just because you're grateful for someone doesn't necessarily mean they know it.

Years ago, I learned one of the greatest principles I've ever heard about gratitude from Andy Stanley. According to Andy, feeling grateful isn't enough. You have to express it. "Unexpressed gratitude," he said, "communicates ingratitude."

Thriving organizations take gratitude and appreciation seriously. It's why one of the core practices of being FOR the team is *appreciate consistently*. As William James once pointed out, "The deepest principle of human nature is the craving to be appreciated."[21]

Far too often, this is missing at work. But again, it's not enough to know how important this is. We must live it out. It's why I want to share one of the very best ways you can create a positive team culture.

The Power of the Handwritten Note

The best ideas are often the simplest. They are often the easiest to ignore as well. The handwritten note is by far one of the best ways to show someone on your team you are FOR them. It's also one of those "important and not urgent" things in life, as Stephen Covey pointed out in *The 7 Habits of Highly Effective People*.[22]

A handwritten note is rarely urgent. A handwritten note is rarely unimportant.

A handwritten note takes some time. It's personal. It rewards the behavior you want repeated. It's a nice thing to do for another human being.

A handwritten note communicates value. It shows the person receiving the note that you really are FOR the team by caring enough to stop what you're doing to write and say thanks.

Something I've noticed is that people usually keep the handwritten notes they receive. I've noticed handwritten notes placed in cubicles and offices and on refrigerator doors. Handwritten notes are rarely tossed away.

My hero in the world of handwritten thank-you notes is the former chairman and CEO of Home Depot, Frank Blake. Frank's story is well-documented, having taken over for Bob Nardelli, who had been fired by the board. At the time, the stock price was stagnant, and there were concerns that customer service wasn't what it had been in the early days. So imagine the world Frank stepped into as chairman and CEO. Your boss is fired. The board hands you the keys and in essence says, "Fix this."

Where do you even begin?

Frank recognized Home Depot didn't have a product issue; Home Depot had a morale issue, one that needed a personal approach. As a result, Frank made a wise move. In fact, it's now legendary. He started writing thank-you notes. Lots of them.

And while handwritten notes weren't the only action Frank took, it's one of the things he credits for the turnaround that Home Depot experienced during his tenure. As you're about to see, it's a powerful example of what can happen when you show the team you are FOR them.

When I say Frank wrote notes, I don't mean he would do this occasionally. He was committed to it. Seriously committed to it.

Frank estimates he wrote a hundred notes each week.

One hundred.

How's that for setting the bar for the rest of us?

Imagine you are an employee of Home Depot, and one day Frank Blake walks into the store. You have a conversation about how things are going. He asks you a few questions, and then he leaves.

A few days later, there's a note in the mail for you. Much to your surprise and delight, it's a note from Frank Blake, thanking you for what you do and how you serve Home Depot customers. Which one of these do you think happens next?

- You toss the note in the trash and move on with your day.
- You save the note and show it to your spouse or friends.

My favorite story about this is when a Home Depot associate saw Frank, thanked him for the note he wrote, and asked him if he could write it again. Frank agreed but asked why the man needed another one.

"When I received your note, everyone said there was no way this was actually handwritten. It must have been computerized. So I put the note under water to test it, and, sure enough, the ink ran. It was real. But the bad news is that I ruined the note."[23]

The reality is that a handwritten note will have a long-lasting impact on the culture and the individual. It's not just a nice thing to do. It is a sincere, practical way to show you are FOR the team, not above the team. Sure, not all of us are CEOs. A note from Frank Blake carries a lot of weight to it. But that shouldn't deter us from doing this, no matter where we land in the organizational structure.

Granted, a hundred notes a week is a high bar. So let's start small.

My challenge to you is to write three thank-you notes a day, five days a week. I'm not very good at math but I'm told that's fifteen notes a week. If I give you two weeks off for vacation, that's fifteen notes a week times fifty weeks, which again I'm told is 750 handwritten notes a year. The reality, though, is that it's not 750 notes. The message of the note will spread to spouses, friends, and families. More people will read these notes than the 750 recipients. As a result, the culture begins to lift. People begin to lift. And as this happens, the rising tide lifts the organization.

Do you think the people who received a note from Frank Blake served Home Depot customers more or less passionately as a result of this? It's one of the secrets of the turnaround success he had there. It's also another example of how to "grow small," as we discussed in section 1.

This one simple exercise, if done consistently, will leave an indelible imprint on the people and culture of your organization. (It will also leave an indelible imprint on your personal brand, which we'll talk about in section 4.)

Handwritten notes are such a big deal that I wanted you to hear directly from Frank on how to do this. In some ways, it's kind of like saying, "Excuse me, Mr. Jordan. Can you teach me how to shoot a basketball?" Frank Blake is the Michael Jordan of thank-you notes. (And yes, I'm looking at you, LeBron fans.)

Here's what I wanted to explore with Frank: How did he decide who should receive a note? What was his system? What did the note say? When did he find the time to write? Did the Home Depot board ever question why he was spending so much time writing thank-you notes? What kind of feedback did he receive from the notes? Did he ever worry about people who didn't receive the notes since he couldn't write everyone? And finally, one hundred?

As we do this, I want to create a three-part system for you based on what we learn from Frank. But before I do, let me reiterate. There may be a part of you that wonders why I'm making such a big deal out of handwritten notes. It all goes back to showing those you work with that you are FOR them. It's a rather sad indictment on the culture of work in our world that something as simple, encouraging, and nice as a handwritten note is bewildering to people. They don't really have a category for it. The initial response is one of skepticism, so we put it under water to see if it's actually real. Handwritten notes exceed the expectations of the team. And as Howard Schultz, founder of Starbucks, has said, "When you exceed the expectations of the team, they exceed the expectations of the customer."[24]

If you dismiss the notion of handwritten notes as a "nice

thing but who has time for that?" you get in line behind the rest of the world.

If you decide to take it seriously, you join a small circle of people like Frank Blake. The reason Frank took this seriously is because he saw a direct connection between handwritten notes and cementing the mission of Home Depot, which is to be the best customer service retailer in the world.

"There is a common saying in business that 'you get what you measure,'" Frank said. "You also get what you celebrate. This is why handwritten notes are so important because one of your jobs is to let people working in your organization understand what you want. The most powerful way to do that is to celebrate them and what they did."[25]

> **IF you dismiss the notion of handwritten notes as a "nice thing but who has time for that?" you get in line behind the rest of the world.**

This is the power of the handwritten note. It both encourages and informs. It casts vision and clarifies the mission. Plus, we all know what it feels like when we receive a handwritten note. This prompts the question, then, *why isn't it happening more often in organizations?*

The answer is simple. We don't have a system to turn good intentions into reality.

Thanks to Frank Blake, now you do.

Frank Blake's Handwritten Note System

1. Develop a System That Delivers Stories

The scale of Home Depot is massive, with 2,285 stores and more than 400,000 associates. The challenge for Frank was trying to consistently find stories to celebrate and thank people. One of his first moves as CEO was to develop a way for each district to find one story to recognize. This story would be passed along to Frank, and the note writing would begin. Another system Frank often followed was to spend time wearing an orange apron and walking around the stores serving customers. He'd observe other associates and how they were serving, and he'd take notes. He was constantly on the search for stories.

A system that has been helpful to me is to ask our team for help. On Sunday evenings, I text the staff at Gwinnett Church and ask them to send me stories of something one of their volunteers did so I can write them a note.

Another way is to eavesdrop in on social media and celebrate the team there. For example, one Sunday I saw this on Instagram.

The caption read: "This, right here, is why I love my @gwinnettchurch family. We truly are all about community, togetherness, and being #ForGwinnett #itsthelittlethings #love"

I reposted it on my Instagram account with this comment: "One of our Guest Services mantras at Gwinnett Church is for each of us to WOW one person every Sunday. It's why I loved this post from @marcie.may.i today on how the Parking Team served her. I'm grateful for volunteers who go the second mile like this. In doing so, you show our guests God is FOR them by how well you SERVE them. #ForGwinnett"

To show the team you are FOR them will require you to have some type of system to collect stories. It's a vital way to turn this from good intention into sustainable reality.

2. Put It on Your Calendar

Frank would write his notes on a weekend afternoon in his office at home. It became an appointment that he consistently kept. *Warning*: appointments like these are easy to cancel because they aren't urgent. One of the reasons Frank was so successful is that he refused to let this happen. He kept this appointment with himself and his note-writing system.

When are you going to write your notes? Don't leave it up to intention. Be specific. Make an appointment. Put it on your calendar. And barring any emergency, don't cancel.

Again, by putting this on the calendar, Frank turned a good intention into reality and sustained it. Like good leaders do.

3. Determine Your Goal

Frank had a goal for one hundred notes a week. Mine is fifteen. (For those of you who are counting at home, Frank is eighty-five times better than me.)

I encourage you to start small. How about one note a day this week for three days? Then build from there.

A few more helpful tips:

Set yourself up for success. I always carry a stack of note cards in my backpack and in the glove compartment of my car. This allows me to leverage moments of downtime, such as waiting in the doctor's office or waiting for someone who's late for an appointment. I can get in a note or two in these moments. It's much more effective than scrolling through Twitter.

The more specific the better. A general thank-you isn't good enough. This is why collecting specific stories are helpful. Stories provide opportunities for you to specifically point out what the team member did and why it connects to the vision and mission of your organization.

Highlight who they are, not just what they did. There is no way to grow a healthy organization with unhealthy people. I know this may make us a bit uncomfortable in the business world, but I firmly believe one of our tasks as leaders is to grow the character and integrity of the teams we serve. While highlighting what a team member did, you can simply add, "This shows your heart, humility, and character. It shows the kind of person you are, and I am honored to be on this team with you."[26]

> A person who feels appreciated will always do more than is expected.

We do ourselves and the places we work for a disservice by underestimating consistent appreciation. A person who feels appreciated will always do more than is expected.

Too Good to Not Be True

Let's revisit the question we introduced at the beginning of this section: What does it *feel* like to work here?

When I mention organizations that make their teams feel believed in and appreciated, I'm often met with a look that seems like I'm expressing some faraway magical place that doesn't truly exist.

No, it's *not* too good to be true. In fact, *it's too good to not be true*. We can be true to the work we've been charged to do by being good to the people who do the work.

Believe abundantly.

Appreciate consistently.

Wouldn't we all want to work at a place that did these two things?

And as you're about to see in the next chapter, it also helps save money.

(Finally I said something that captured the attention of the accountants.)

HOW TO HAVE
Better Meetings

Here's an idea. Post a running scoreboard counting the amount of money being spent on overhead at each meeting. At the conclusion, everyone looks at the scoreboard and asks the question, "Was this a good use of the money we just spent?"

Okay, maybe that's a bit too much.

And yet it illustrates the point that meetings are one of the largest, often hidden costs of any organization.

To become better organizations, we need to become better at meetings. When we become better at meetings, we become better at intentionally developing the team.

Let me explain. In recent years, *leadership development* has become quite the buzz phrase in organizations, and rightly so. Thriving organizations develop their teams. This often takes the form of retreats, off-sites, and conferences.

And when we return, we go right back into meetings.

One of the best ways to intentionally develop your teams is to do it within the existing framework of systems already happening, such as meetings. It's why I want to focus in on meetings as an example of how to *develop intentionally*.

Generally speaking, there are two types of people in the world: those who like meetings, and those who lie and *say* they like meetings. (I'm just kidding. Sort of.) But in reality, there's only one kind of person in the world—we all go to meetings. They don't have to be formalized or be a gathering in a boardroom. Sometimes meetings are held around a dinner table, at the coffee shop, or by video chat.

And while meetings have often been one of the most criticized aspects of organizational life, it would be impossible to have a thriving organization without some sort of gathering for communication, vision casting, and clarity.

That's why one of the best ways an organization can show they are FOR the team is to simply have better meetings. Sure, information is important. But *inspiration* is always better. Meetings are an opportunity for both.

Often, the problem isn't the meeting. The problem is that organizations don't often *prepare* for the meeting. It's on the calendar. It's just not on purpose. When meetings "just happen," organizations are burning money, often failing to count the cost of the overhead in the room.

For a number of years, I've helped coach business presenters and pastors with their presentations. The very first principle we start with is, *"The better you prepare, the better you present."* It seems rather obvious, but the reality is that many presenters have never been taught how to prepare. As a result, procrastination often wins out.

I remember one time I was coaching an entrepreneur who was preparing a presentation where he was asking potential investors for funding. I told him his presentation was too long. He needed to make it shorter, and to do that, he would have to work longer on it. Ironically, shorter presentations require more work and preparation. Less is more. It's not just true with presentations; it's also true with meetings.

I have a hunch that many meetings will be led this week by people who are not prepared. As a result, the mythical running scoreboard counting the overheard costs will click through a lot of wasted dollars.

This doesn't have to be our story though. We can battle against procrastination through preparation. Preparation is where the magic really happens.

I believe the better you prepare for the meeting, the better the meeting will be. It's one of the most practical ways to show you are FOR the team because you are valuing their time.

A point of confession though. I didn't come by this naturally. I'm not a person who loves meetings. I could blame it on being an introvert, but the reality is, I just wasn't as prepared for the meetings I led as I should have been. As a result, I wasn't serving the team very well in these meetings. There was no specified goal for the meeting. The team showed up because I asked them to put it on their calendar.

It took me a while, but I slowly began to realize that one of the best ways to show the team I was FOR them was to spend time preparing for the meeting, not just showing up for the meeting.

I eventually realized the better I prepare for the meeting, the better the meeting will be. A few years ago, my friend David Farmer showed me something he calls "the Big L Leader."[27]

The Big L Leader has three components:

- Thought Leader
- People Leader
- Project Leader

One of the ways David shows his team he's for them is to help them grow in each of these areas. His theory is that as an individual grows in each area, they grow into a Big L Leader, moving closer to their potential. I think he's right.

When I saw this, I immediately wondered if it could be a framework for the meetings I led. Since it applies to individuals, could it also apply to teams? If a team grows in each of these areas, could the team move closer to its collective potential?

I also had a hunch that most meetings focus primarily on projects, which is the WHAT of the organization. As a result, most meetings rarely talk about the WHO (people) and the WHY (thought). This means that WHAT (projects) often receives more focus than WHO and WHY. I think that's the opposite of the way it should be.

Three years ago, I decided to give it a try. I started framing my meetings around these three sections, with the corresponding questions under each one as a guide.

- **Thought Leadership:** How can we see and shape the future?
- **People Leadership:** Am I growing? Are we growing?
- **Project Leadership:** How can we be more effective and efficient at the same time?

Under each section would be the pertinent information related to the three. For example, under Thought Leadership, I usually bring an insight from the current book I'm reading. Under People Leadership, we talk about our culture, what it feels like to work around here, and other issues related to staffing. And then we save the last for Project Leadership, which is usually a list of items we need to make decisions on and become aware of as a leadership team.

If you think this looks simple, you're right. But remember, *simple wins*. One of the best ways to show the team you're for them is to simply show up prepared. How many meetings have you been in where there's no agenda? Imagine how much money is wasted by not fully leveraging the meeting. Imagine if people actually looked forward to meetings. If this happened, organizations would stop burning so much money in meetings.

While there are countless ideas to intentionally develop the team, few provide the regularity and necessity that meetings do.

When an organization gets better at meetings, the meetings make the organization better. It also saves the organization money. It's why I still think someone should be brave enough to install a running scoreboard in meeting rooms to count the overhead cost. Anyone want to go first?

Where the
BEST IDEAS
Are Hiding

CHAPTER 13

Before we go any further, here's a brief recap on how to design a FOR culture:

- Believe abundantly.
- Appreciate consistently.
- Develop intentionally.

The next one helps us locate a place where many of the best ideas in our organization are hiding. This is another tangible advantage of creating a FOR culture because it increases the likelihood of innovation. When the team knows you are FOR them, they will feel more emboldened to speak up and provide feedback.

Here's a truth that's common to all of us, regardless of the kind of work we do: innovation often hides *within* the organization.

In other words, there are great ideas in the minds of the team that are often untapped. Sometimes you don't need to look for innovation. Sometimes you simply need to listen for it.

A great example of what can happen when there is space for a team to share ideas is the work of Cheryl Bachelder, former CEO of Popeyes Louisiana Kitchen. Cheryl led one of the best turnaround stories in recent business history.

She began as Popeyes CEO in November 2007. Prior to this, Cheryl had more than thirty-five years of experience with Yum Brands, Domino's Pizza, RJR Nabisco, the Gillette Company, and the Procter & Gamble Company. In other words, Cheryl knows what she's doing.

And yet she did something unusual. Rather than start making fast decisions, she went on what she describes as a listening tour. She traveled extensively and met with franchisees, restaurant general managers, employees, and customers.

"When I joined Popeyes, there was a lack of trust between our franchisees and the company. Customer satisfaction scores were low. Annual sales were declining. We were in a tough spot," Cheryl said.

What she learned was hard to see on a spreadsheet, but it was without a doubt impacting what she saw on a spreadsheet.

"The listening tour gave me a guide to know how to best build trust with the team," Cheryl said. "There were many things I heard that I had already suspected, but there was also quite a lot that was new to me. It was the foundation of what was to come."

One of the ways she did this was by asking the team questions and then following up with these three powerful words: "Tell me more."

"Tell me more" is so powerful because it shows humility, curiosity, and value. This simple approach led to several innovations. Here are two of them.

"We had no innovation pipeline for new products," Cheryl

told me. "One of the things I wanted to understand is how hard would it be to generate food innovation within our restaurants. So I asked the general managers of our restaurants, 'Do you love our food?' They all said they definitely loved the food. Then I asked them, 'So what do you make for lunch?'

"They went on these long explanations of innovative recipes using ingredients that were *already* in the stores. Then I asked them to tell me more. 'Do you think customers would like what you've created?' They told me they had never thought about it. This is when it occurred to me that we needed to tap into the innovation that is already happening in the back of our restaurants."

Cheryl used the same approach when she asked the team of Popeyes franchisees, "When do we do our best work together?" First of all, this is a fantastic question that we should all ask the team. Second, it led Cheryl to an insight she said she would have never had.

"WHEN do we do our best work together?"

"Oh, that's easy to answer," one franchisee said. "It's when you don't bring a PowerPoint presentation to the meeting."

"Tell me more," Cheryl said.

"The very fact that you have a PowerPoint presentation shows you already have the answer," the franchisee continued. "All we are there for is to tell you we like your answer. That's not a great way to collaborate."

In that moment, Cheryl smiled because she knew he was exactly correct.

"Tell me more," she said. "What would it look like if we eliminated the PowerPoint approach and worked differently?"

"You would show up with an empty flip chart and two markers," he said. "Then we would solve the problem together."

Cheryl said she learned a powerful lesson from the franchisees. "They were teaching us what listening looked like in real life. It looks like a blank piece of paper and an open mind to hear what others have to say. You simply can't hear a great new idea or the solution to a problem if you're busy talking. When you collaborate on the answer together, then you're ready to act on the plan together."

In this example, Cheryl shows us a highly effective and cost-efficient pathway to innovation. We can unearth the great ideas that already exist within our organizations if we'll *listen actively*. Yes, we need to listen carefully, but ultimately we need to listen actively, collaborate on the idea or solution, and then have the courage to act on what we heard.

How can we *listen actively*?

- Ask great questions.
- Listen for insights.
- Act on what you hear.

At the heart of listening actively is a sincere belief in the team. Cheryl demonstrated this belief in the team by choosing humility over power, listening over talking, action over passivity.

And sure, all of this sounds nice, but what about the bottom-line results? I'm glad you asked.

In Cheryl's eight years as CEO, Popeyes' market cap increased from less than $300 million to more than $1.3 billion. Annual sales exceeded $3.1 billion. That's a lot of listening. That's a lot of innovation. That's a lot of chicken.

CHAPTER 14

A Vision Worth
WORKING FOR

I t was the first and only time I have ever done a stage-dive after giving a talk. I was speaking to Boosterthon. (Since you might doubt the stage-dive story, I've included the photo.)

Stage-diving wasn't my idea. It was Chris Carneal's, the founder of Boosterthon. When I finished my talk, the chant began. "Jeff! Jeff! Jeff!" Everyone stood up chanting my name, which was code for "we are ready to pass you from the front to the back." It was their way of saying thank you.

The energy in this company is hard to describe. You feel it when you walk into their offices, or when they're passing you from the front of the room to the back.

Boosterthon helps schools raise money. That's their mission. Their vision is CTW, which stands for "Change the World."

Helping schools raise money is really nice, but *changing the world*? Really? How does that work? Stay tuned.

The other fascinating aspect about Boosterthon is that it is led and run primarily by millennials—you know, the often criticized and maligned group when it comes to the workplace.

Boosterthon is a case study of what can happen when you show people, no matter their age, that you are FOR them.

What Chris has done is connect a practical and helpful mission (help schools raise money) with a huge vision (CTW). A huge vision without a pathway for making it come true is rhetoric. It sounds like a campaign promise that we all know won't happen. However, a practical mission that can be accomplished with no lasting purpose becomes a job.

"I believe everyone wants to live for something beyond themselves and to work for something that makes a difference," Chris said. "I love creating opportunities like that for people."[28]

By connecting mission and vision, Chris and the team at Booster Enterprises are giving their team something every person wants: a desire to make a difference and to live for a story that's bigger than us as individuals.

This is one of the best gifts you can give people on the team—a vision worth working for. It is something that is bigger than you and me. It *requires* us.

Chris is the son of a teacher. He saw firsthand how many teachers often pay for school supplies out of their own pockets to help students. He also saw schools raising money by selling products. He believed there could be a better way.

"Instead of selling candy bars and wrapping paper, we decided to help students in three ways: fitness, leadership, and character," Chris said. "Could we create a way for schools to raise money *and* increase the fitness, leadership, and character of students during the process?"

Within that question, the nucleus of CTW becomes real. For example, Boosterthon currently serves three thousand schools. While that's a very strong reach, Chris quickly points out that there are one hundred thousand elementary schools in the United States alone.

"We're only at 3 percent impact at this point. We have a huge opportunity before us," he said. "It's why I believe Boosterthon provides an opportunity for someone to be a part of a larger story. Imagine if one day we can serve one hundred thousand schools. That would be of epic, CTW proportions. Who wouldn't want to be a part of that?"

In other words, the vision is so much bigger than Chris. It's so much bigger than a few people. It needs an *us*.

Once you have that kind of vision, it leads to a simple, powerful recruiting question: "Do you want to become a part of *us*, because we *need* you?"

Maybe the reality about millennials isn't that they are lazy. Maybe the reality is that they are bored. They aren't in it to sell stuff. They want to know that what they're selling is leading to something good. Selling stuff is fine, but once you've tasted purpose, it's hard to just sell stuff. Sure, Boosterthon sells fun runs. But in actuality, what they're selling is *purpose*, not just to their clients but to their team. And when you sell purpose to your team, a compelling purpose that requires a committed, bought-in *us*, well, the energy is palpable. You can feel it.

You may even be cheered to stage-dive.

While I'm not suggesting stage-diving needs to necessarily become part of your culture, I do believe that signs of joy, fun, and enthusiasm are natural ingredients of a place that is truly FOR the team. Again it goes back to the question, "What does it *feel* like to work here?"

"Culture is what I love the most," Chris said. "I want an environment that is fun and memorable. Most of all, we want our culture to reinforce our mission and vision."

And that leads me to the final piece of designing a FOR culture: *live repeatedly*.

One of the ways you reinforce the mission and vision is to say it over, and over and over and over again. Leaders are repeaters.

It's why language that communicates the vision is important. It's why all of us need to continue to work at becoming better communicators. Eventually leadership comes with a microphone. (More on this in section 4.)

Most of all, we need to live out the vision in our own lives. Repeatedly. Daily. In fact, let me give one of the best examples I've ever seen that shows the power of putting vision on repeat and learning how to live repeatedly.

"My Pleasure"

If you've ever been to a Chick-fil-A restaurant and said thank you, odds are very high you've heard the team member reply back not with "you're welcome" but with "my pleasure."

I remember when this started. I was on staff and attending the corporate convention when Truett shared the story of the time he was staying at a Ritz-Carlton. When he said thank you to a staff person, they replied back with "my pleasure."

He immediately thought, *That's so much better than "you're welcome." We should do this at Chick-fil-A!*

And an idea was born.

Since then, these two words have become a vital part of the Chick-fil-A customer service culture. It's one of the primary ways Chick-fil-A has distinguished itself from their competitors. The fact that Truett would bring a phrase from a high-end hotel chain and introduce it to a quick-service restaurant chain is a lesson for us all.

Honestly, it's more than a little surprising. In some quick-service restaurants, "you're welcome" would be surprising to hear in and of itself. It's a little surprising to have high-end caliber service at a low-price point establishment.

That's the beauty of an idea like this.

Great ideas elevate.

Great ideas elevate the mission. Great ideas elevate the purpose. Great ideas elevate customer interaction. But most important of all, great ideas elevate the people on the team.

By comparing Chick-fil-A service to the Ritz-Carlton, Truett elevated the standard. He didn't look around at the usual competition in his industry. He went outside of it and found an organization that was leading the way in customer service.

It was no small thing on Truett's part to go from hearing "my pleasure" to thinking, *We can do this too!* It may seem small. It's not.

It required something in Truett to make the leap from ideation to implementation.

And isn't that the challenge? From ideation to implementation. It's not about having a great idea. It's about executing that great idea. It sounds easy.

It wasn't.

We have an illusion when it comes to CEOs and business

founders like Truett Cathy. We think it's easier for them than it is for us. *Somehow,* we think, *they've been blessed in ways we haven't, so life is just a bit easier for them.* (Sure, there are strengths they have that can't be ignored, but I dare say few CEOs say their role is easy.)

The reason I bring this up is it's easy to assume, for example, that Truett announced the idea of "my pleasure" at the corporate convention and then everything fell magically into place. Instantly.

That's not what happened. It took time. Some estimate it took a few years for this to flow throughout the organization. That's not surprising when you consider that Chick-fil-A operates more than 2,300 restaurants, opening a new one each week across the United States.

When initiatives like this aren't going as fast as the CEO would like, they are often tempted to power up. Eventually you hear that dreaded word *mandate.*

There's a better approach. Granted, it takes more time, but instead of mandating, you put the vision on repeat. *You live repeatedly.*

Truett didn't get angry. He just kept saying it.

"When customers say thank you, let's say my pleasure."

He said it over and over and over.

And over.

And over again.

And while I'm at it, let me repeat myself: *leaders are repeaters.*

It would be nice to live in a world where we say something once and everyone remembers it. I don't live in that world. Neither do you.

Vision rarely repeated is quickly forgotten.

The reason you've heard "my pleasure" at Chick-fil-A is because Truett put the message on repeat. Yes, he believed the people at Chick-fil-A could rise to the level of service like the Ritz-Carlton. But he also knew the daily challenges of running a business. The urgent pushes the important down and clamors for attention. For the important to stick, the important has to rise up, dust itself off, and keep at it.

You've got to stay on message. You've got to put the vision on repeat.

Whenever I hear "my pleasure" at Chick-fil-A, I ask myself this question: "Am I repeating the vision as much as Truett did?" Whenever you hear this from now on, I'm asking you to ask yourself the same question.

Living the vision repeatedly elevates the team. It breathes life and encouragement into the culture of the organizations we serve. Chris Carneal is right. There is something in all of us that wants to work for something bigger than ourselves. By repeating the vision, you're giving those you work with an amazing gift—the gift of *purpose*.

As the old saying goes, "The main thing is keeping the main thing the main thing." The challenge for many organizations and teams is confusion over what the main thing actually is. If there is confusion in the office space, there will be confusion in the marketplace. The reason is simple. Organizations drift toward complexity, especially growing ones, and we stop repeating the vision. This happens because we stop personally living it. Eventually we no longer work for a purpose. We work

IF there is confusion in the office space, there will be confusion in the marketplace.

at a job. People easily leave jobs. It's hard to walk away from purpose.

This is why one of the best ways you can show you are FOR the team is to put vision on repeat. Gone are the days of saying it once and having it stick. (Did those days ever exist?) To help you accomplish this, I want to give you the best vision question to ask yourself. It's also a great vision question to give the team.

The Vision Question

David Salyers spent more than thirty years in marketing at Chick-fil-A. He is the best marketing strategist I've ever been around. He hired me at Chick-fil-A.

In my early months there, David and I would visit Chick-fil-A stores together. Our goal was to serve the operator by helping him or her build sales. It was in this setting that I learned a question from David that has helped me ever since.

After spending some time with the operator and hearing about their business, David would ask a simple question: "What did you do today to build your business?"

Often, the answers would be, "Last week I had a huge catering order." "I'm planning on doing direct mail next month." "I'm leasing a billboard in a few weeks just down the road."

All of these are fine answers. None answered David's question.

One word in his question made all the difference: "What did you do *today* to build your business?"

Building your business is a daily task. It never goes away.

The running of the business often overtakes the building of the business.

When I learned this question from David, I thought it could apply to vision casting as well. After all, one of the best ways to build your business daily is to remind everyone daily of the vision behind the business.

Here's what I know about the people you work with and what I know about you. Each of you is on a pursuit toward meaning. I am too.

We want our days to matter. We are searching for meaningful, purposeful work. This is why vision needs to be on repeat. With this in mind, I modified David's question slightly and began asking it of myself and our team at Gwinnett Church.

"What did we do *today* to cast vision for our church?"

The vision question is like an alarm clock. It nudges us and says, "Welcome to today, another opportunity to live repeatedly what's most important. What will you do today to keep the main thing the main thing? What will you do today to cast vision for the organization?"

Gwinnett Church

This question becomes even more powerful when everyone begins to ask it. It's why we gave these stickers out to everyone at Gwinnett Church to place on their laptops. It's not a huge idea, but it's something they see almost every day.

When a team answers this question repeatedly, the vision lives repeatedly.

Designing a FOR Culture

Let's do a brief recap: this section is about the opportunity we all have to be FOR the people we work with or report to or those who report to us. Being FOR the team isn't touchy-feely, unless you think a healthy bottom line is touchy-feely.

The reason for this is simple: customers experience your culture. An organization can fake it for a while, but eventually if the team doesn't feel cared for, they won't take care of the customer. *How the team is treated is eventually how the customer is treated.*

There's a phrase for what happens when a team doesn't feel cared for and when they aren't served well. It's called "high turnover rates."

High staff turnover results in lower sales.

Again, dismissing this as touchy-feely is dismissing the importance of the bottom line. Fantastic products with a bad work culture will eventually produce a bad product. And bad products don't sell very well.

It's why the overall principle about being FOR the team is one about your culture: *culture is created by default or by design.*

Here's the road map on how to design a FOR culture:

- Believe abundantly.
- Appreciate consistently.
- Develop intentionally.

- Listen actively.
- Live repeatedly.

From my observations and experience, this is the heartbeat of thriving organizations. We all know the difference it made in our lives to have someone believe in us, appreciate us, develop us, and listen to us, all while offering an opportunity to be a part of something bigger than us.

If this sounds familiar, it's because it is. It's not a new idea, but it's a mostly forgotten one: "Do to others as you would have them do to you" (Luke 6:31).

That's how to be FOR the team.

SECTION 3

FOR THE COMMUNITY

We should be about more than just selling chicken. We should be a part of our customers' lives and the communities in which we serve.

TRUETT CATHY

CHAPTER 15

GOOD FOR
Goodness' Sake

"If our church closed down, would the community even notice?" This is the question I posed in the early days of Gwinnett Church. It's admittedly an odd question in the start-up days, but I wanted it to help guide our thinking. I wanted us to add so much value to the community that if someday we decided to close the church, the community would protest and try to keep us open.

I would want the mayor, school principals and teachers, business owners, and parents and students to call and say, "You *can't* close! Our community needs this church to stay open."

The problem with many churches, nonprofits, and businesses is that if they closed down tomorrow, the community around them wouldn't know it. The organization's purpose never flowed beyond the walls of the organization.

If the ultimate goal is staying in business, you won't. As the Havas Group pointed out in section 1, the world is looking for organizations that are making our lives better and making the world a better place to live.

Granted, I get it if you're in the start-up phase, fighting to make payroll. You're trying to survive another day. I completely understand. Yet there still needs to be a driving, larger purpose, even from the beginning.

It's why being FOR people in addition to customers and the team is vitally important. You can't just talk about being FOR people; you have to show it. If not, organizations can slip into the "all about us" marketing strategy.

Nowhere is this more evident than in the marketing approach of the mobile communications industry with companies such as AT&T, Sprint, Verizon, and the like. Talk about soulless advertising. We are in the midst of the greatest communications change in the last five hundred years. The potential of how this may positively or negatively impact our lives is staggering. Sure, it's already having an impact, but these organizations could help set the tone, be the standard, and lead the way. They could model how to use technology to make a difference, showing teens how to avoid the anxiety that is building among them due in part to technology, as an example.

Instead, it's all about pricing, how much better they are than the competitors—the usual boring approach. Do pricing and having a great product matter? Absolutely, but so does *purpose*. I see no "larger than us" purpose or vision when observing their marketing strategy. The primary focus is the business.

For example, when's the last time someone said to you, "I am so grateful for AT&T because . . ." "Have you seen what Sprint did to help make the world a better place?" "Verizon helped teach my teen to manage her screen time by . . ."

Instead, Sprint starts using the former Verizon guy in their advertising, and the beat goes on.

We can do better than this. We can build companies and

create marketing strategies that solve problems and lift up people and communities, while at the same time growing the bottom line. This isn't some altruistic plea that demeans profit and growth. Far from it. For far too long, we've assumed we can't have both. In today's world, where the customer is in charge like never before, they are watching and waiting to reward the companies that actually do this.

Take Domino's Pizza, for instance. In June 2018, Domino's launched its Paving for Pizza community initiative. We probably all know what it's like to be driving with a pizza in the front seat, hit a pothole, and watch the pizza go flying. Domino's decided it would be a win-win for communities and their customers if they fixed a few potholes around the country. They launched PavingforPizza.com and invited communities to submit requests for Domino's to pave the potholes free of charge to the community.

"Within the first couple of weeks, we had submissions from every state," said Dan Corken, who was a vice president and executive producer for CP + B, Domino's ad agency at that time.

Courtesy of Domino's Pizza

"That was something we identified as an interesting opportunity for us, to just keep going."[29]

In two weeks, the campaign had generated 100,00 site visits, 31,000 zip code registrations from all 50 states, 700 media stories, and 100,000 Twitter mentions. It was number one on Reddit. The campaign ad has now been viewed more than 600,000 times on YouTube.

This is a classic example of how a win for a community can be a win for a business. Sure, Domino's could have created a campaign about how much better they are than their competitors—but . . . *yawn*. Who really cares that you think you're better than your competition? Show us what you're doing for us. Show us who you're FOR and not who you're against. Give us a reason to talk positively about your organization because when you do, we'll become a sales force for free.

In this case, Domino's showed us they are for local communities. You can't pave every pothole, but you can pave some. And the fact that they would even try triggered a response from a wider community beyond their customer base. Domino's wasn't just impacting pizza eaters; they were impacting people. They were doing good for goodness' sake. And again, doing good is increasingly good for business.

As I stated earlier, nonprofit leaders can learn a lot from business leaders. In this section, we're going to see how business leaders can learn from nonprofit leaders by expanding organizational impact beyond the customer base.

When you widen the circle of impact, it leads to a priceless, tangible result every organization is secretly striving for—*brand loyalty*. Loyalty is how your organization endears itself to people, causing them to believe in what you're doing and support you as you do it. Loyalty is how your organization makes them feel—giving them a sense of pride, appreciation, and gratitude. Loyalty is when people ask with wonder, "Why would they do this when there is seemingly no inherent self-interest here?" Like fixing potholes.

Here's how this works: When people who aren't your customers speak positively about your organization to people who are your customers, it increases loyalty on the part of the customers. People want to feel good about the companies and organizations they support. One of the ways to do this is to do good for goodness' sake, no strings attached.

For example, I've had non-coffee drinkers tell me how much they admire Starbucks for being one of the first US retailers to offer comprehensive health coverage to full-time and part-time employees and their families.

This, of course, brings up a very important question: Is there really such a thing as a "non-coffee drinker"?

Crazy, isn't it?

Here's another question to consider: What is your organization doing that is so noteworthy and good that even noncustomers are talking about it?

The logical question is, "Why should we be interested in what noncustomers think?"

That's easy to answer. It shows you have a far deeper purpose than just staying in business. As I pointed out earlier, if the ultimate goal is staying in business, you probably won't. If there isn't a larger impact than the business, then there is no compelling vision because it's just all about us or about those at the top of the organization.

When there is no compelling purpose, the team hits the

snooze button more often. However, when there is a compelling purpose beyond the organization, people get out of bed more quickly. There's a reason waiting for them at work. Again, it's why being FOR the community—the world even—must be somewhere on the radar of everyone in the organization. We aren't just here to sell stuff; we're here to make a difference.

Here's another way to say this: *Selling is transactional. Loyalty is relational.*

This isn't a criticism of selling. (In fact, we're going to talk about purpose in the purchase in this section.) Instead, the point is loyalty will actually lead to more sales.

The good news is creating this kind of loyalty doesn't have to be mysterious, expensive, or nonstrategic. Loyalty can flow through the customers and the team to a wider community. This is where the magic happens. This is where making a bigger difference happens. And the next chapter shows us the pathway to get there.

The Pathway to
BRAND LOYALTY

CHAPTER 16

The pathway to brand loyalty leads through four mileposts:

1. Belonging leads to buying
2. Purpose in the purchase
3. Influence beyond the business
4. Impact from the business

FOR: THE COMMUNITY

If there isn't a purpose bigger than the business, the business won't get any bigger.

I want to lean slightly more toward our business readers in this section, but all of these apply to nonprofit organizations as well. It's easy to think that with nonprofits, purpose and product are intertwined. What we're going to discover is the same is true for businesses.

When your product and purpose are intertwined, the more products you sell, the more purpose you have. This is the future—organizations that create value and meaning by being and doing. It's part of your ethos, heartbeat, and emotional makeup. You don't have to convince us to buy. We're smart. We can figure this out. Show us who and what you're FOR, and we'll take it from there.

Here's how to show us:

Belonging Leads to Buying

We all want to belong.

One of the best lessons I've learned at North Point Ministries is to help people feel *a sense of belonging before they believe*. Belonging is a fundamental human need that is often overlooked and untapped by most organizations.

In their work, sociologists Roy Baumeister and Mark Leary have identified belonging as a desire that has no cultural or geographic boundaries. It is a common human bond that all of us desire.[30] It's why phrases such as "Bulldog Nation" are about more than just college football. It's about belonging. There are people who belong to Bulldog Nation who have never attended a single class at the University of Georgia. And yet they drive around with a Bulldog license plate on the front of their car, buy T-shirts and hats, and give UGA birthday gifts. Too often, businesses define their customers only as "those who went to school here." Nonprofits define their constituency only as "those who donated." This kind of thinking limits the potential scope of impact, both for the organization and the community.

Creating a sense of belonging > getting someone to buy something.

When people feel a sense of belonging, they aren't just buying a product; they are buying purpose. As a result, each purchase creates an even deeper emotional bond with the customer.

This is why a purpose beyond just the customer and team is so important. The product is a means to an end—which is the purpose. Sadly, the reason purpose beyond the customer doesn't exist is because too often there isn't one. As a result, we play a tightrope game with our margins through discounting and competing on price. Discounting may spark a quick burst of sales, but it rarely has staying power, and it certainly has limits.

Discounting doesn't grow margins like purpose does.

This leads to a few important questions for you and the organization to think through:

DISCOUNTING doesn't grow margins like purpose does.

- What problem is our organization trying to solve for the community?
- How are we making the community better?
- Why should the community care if our organization starts to struggle?
- What larger purpose do customers or participants belong to when they support our organization?

- What would we like to be known FOR in the community?
- What *are* we known FOR in the community?
- Where are we doing good for goodness' sake, no strings attached?

Searching for a Community to Belong

I know, I know. This sounds a bit too altruistic, but we're talking about a fundamental human need—the need to belong to something bigger than ourselves. When we ignore this, we ignore a basic human need and overlook the opportunity to impact more people. Remember, if there isn't a purpose bigger than the business, the business won't get any bigger.

Don't forget, people are searching for a community to belong to. Not just a physical neighborhood, but something deeper and even more tangible than that.

For example, when we were building the campus for the first Gwinnett Church location, city officials said we could post a "Coming Soon" sign on the property. "Gwinnett Church, coming soon in January 2015," is typically what a sign like this would say. It's exactly what I did *not* want to do. I didn't want our very first message to the community to be exclusive to people interested in church.

I wanted the message to create a sense of belonging, whether or not they were interested in church. I wanted our first message to speak to a larger community—the entire community. I wanted the message to convey, *We're building this FOR the community.*

It's why instead of saying something about Gwinnett Church, we simply put this sign on the property:

Gwinnett Church

Courtesy of Dorrin Johnson

Shortly after the sign went up, a funny and interesting thing started happening. People stopped and got their picture taken by the sign.

This is the power of belonging, of being FOR a larger community than just your customer base.

Occasionally someone would ask, "How are they going to know what's being built? How will they know it's a church?"

"Exactly," I'd reply. We wanted to create a conversation with the community.

We received tweets like this: "Does anyone know what's going on at Peachtree Industrial Boulevard? #ForGwinnett."

We would retweet this and simply respond by saying, "We do. ☺"

We wanted to let our entire community know we are FOR

them. We weren't trying to shine a spotlight on ourselves. We were trying to connect with our community, whether or not they would ever set foot in our church.

The larger you can draw your circle of influence, the wider your potential impact spreads. The reason many employees feel a lack of purpose in their job is that they're unsure of the real purpose of the organization. Understanding the power of belonging allows the purpose of the organization to flow to a wider community, while anchoring the team to it as well. Belonging is one of those intangible qualities that is hard to see on a spreadsheet. But it has a powerful impact on what eventually shows up on the spreadsheet.

Writer Tara Isabella Burton helps us discover this in her fascinating VOX article, "CrossFit Is My Church."[31] In the piece, she talks about the search for belonging and meaning for the "nones." This is the growing demographic that does not identify with a religion. They check the "none" box when asked. One-third of adults identify themselves this way.

However, Ms. Burton points out they're still searching for community. She references the research by Casper ter Kuile, a researcher at Harvard Divinity School and the executive director at On Being's Impact Lab. In a 2015 study, ter Kuile and coauthor Angie Thurston explored how millennials are finding community and belonging in the absence of organized religion.

It was more than a little surprising that their research led them to fitness classes, specifically places like CrossFit and SoulCycle. It wasn't just about fitness; it was about belonging.

"People come because they want to lose weight or gain muscle strength, but they stay for the community," ter Kuile said. "It's really the relationships that keep them coming back."

Ter Kuile added, "We keep saying, 'Meaning-making is a growth industry,' especially as we see more automation and robots and AI and VR and all that stuff. Brands that can offer meaningful experiences of belonging and becoming are going to keep growing.

"How do I feel in a world of isolation? How do I feel truly connected to myself, to people around me, and how do I become the person that I feel called to be? Brands that can help people do those two things are going to see huge success."[32]

FOR Visalia

This explains, in part, the growth that Neighborhood Church in Visalia, California, is experiencing. "A few years ago, we asked ourselves the question, 'If Neighborhood Church disappeared, would anyone care?'" said Kelly Thomas, executive pastor. "We realized the answer was no. We were inwardly focused. It was about us."

The Neighborhood Church team decided it was time for a different approach. "We saw what was happening with other churches as they were implementing the FOR initiative and decided this was consistent with who we wanted to be as a church. FOR helps us clarify who we are and what we're about. I've discovered you can't talk about vision too much, and we leverage this to describe our DNA—we are FOR Visalia."[33]

It's important to note that 82 percent of people who attend Neighborhood Church are under the age of forty, the fastest-growing segment of the nones. Leveraging the FOR approach, according to Kelly, is definitely appealing to a younger demographic and the next generation.

"The really cool thing about this is we are becoming known as a church that invests in and helps our community," Kelly said. "People who don't go to our church are commenting positively about the church. We think that's a huge win."

An example is an article that was published in their local newspaper. Here's a part of what the reporter wrote about Neighborhood Church when people started asking questions about FOR Visalia:

> If you've been driving around town lately you've probably seen small round bumper magnets with two words—For Visalia.
>
> You may have asked, "What is 'For Visalia'?" Or, "Should I be 'For Visalia'?" One local church has the answer.
>
> "Imagine a city where the people who lived in that city were all committed to doing something in some small way to make their block better, their neighborhood better, their schools better, their city better," said Forrest Jenan, lead pastor at Neighborhood Church in Visalia. "There's a million ways that it could happen."
>
> Neighborhood Church has one simple solution, be For Visalia.[34]

Neighborhood Church has created a sense of belonging far beyond just their church. It's the kind of belonging and meaning discussed in Casper ter Kuile's study.

What would it look like for a business or nonprofit to follow this example? To create a larger sense of belonging and meaning far beyond just talking about the business? This is crucial because, as ter Kuile pointed out, "meaning-making is a growth industry." To get there, though, you're going to have to understand the power of FOMO.

A Basic Fear

The power of belonging taps into a fear we all have: FOMO—the fear of missing out. It's true that people want to deeply belong to something. It's also true, maybe even more so, that people don't want to miss out on something. All of us want to be invited to the party. The question, then, is, "What party is my organization throwing that people can belong to?" If people aren't participating in your organization, maybe it's because they don't think they are missing out on something? What is it that your organization offers that could create FOMO and belonging? Remember, belonging and FOMO are two sides of the same coin.

Have you ever noticed when a particular team starts winning, no matter where you live, you suddenly start seeing that team's logo everywhere? It's on flags outside of homes and cars, T-shirts, license plates, and the like. Some call this "jumping on the bandwagon," which may be true, but it illustrates a much deeper need within us. We want to tell the world, "I belong to them." We don't want to miss out on the party.

This is no small thing. It's a deep longing in every single person. The question, then, is, "How do we leverage this so we can reach and impact more people?"

When you create a sense of belonging, you are being FOR the community. You are saying, "We stand for something bigger than ourselves. We're here FOR you. Come join us."

Do you see the contrast in those last two sentences?

"We're here FOR you. Come join us."

It's not about us. It's about you. So come join us.

The question, then, is, "Do I have something to offer that's worth belonging to? Will people experience FOMO if they aren't a part of what we're doing?"

This is the power of building a community of people who aren't around because of the product and price point. Sure, this may attract them there, but it won't usually keep them there. Thriving organizations understand how to transition people from benefiting from the mission to participating in the mission.

Does your community know your mission? Do they know how you're going to make us better? Why should we personally care if your business starts to struggle? What's the word on the street about your organization? How is your organization making things better, regardless of whether I participate or buy? This is the difference between building a community and a customer base. A customer base can be fickle; a community of believers is loyal.

THRIVING organizations understand how to transition people from benefiting from the mission to participating in the mission.

For example, Harley-Davidson has built a loyal, passionate community. They aren't customers; they're family. Harley-Davidson isn't out to bash the competition or compete on price. They have a driving purpose that shows up before and after the point of purchase. It allows them to connect the daily grind of the business with the larger purpose of the vision, all while impacting more and more people—those who participate and even those who currently don't.

It may be important to note that I don't own a motorcycle. When I was a kid, I had a small wreck on a motorcycle trying to be like my hero Evel Knievel. At that point, I decided it would be safer to have basketball heroes. And yet I have an affection and appreciation for Harley-Davidson because I know they're striving to add value to the lives of people. When people who aren't customers appreciate and are grateful for what you're doing, it will reinforce the mission and purpose to those who are.

Purpose in the Purchase

Here's the three-step process Harley-Davidson uses to put purpose in the purchase, and how you can too. As you're about to see, it's not just the moment of purchase that matters or the time someone participates in a nonprofit. That's just one part of the purchase. It's just one part of the participation. When an organization understands all three movements, it creates a deep sense of belonging. When this happens, a wider circle of influence begins to flow well beyond the current participants because it gives them a sense of belonging. In turn, they tell others about it, allowing you once again to leverage a sales force for free.

Before

Harley-Davidson describes the company in six words. And not one of those words includes *motorcycle* in the description.

We fulfill dreams of personal freedom.

In these six words, Harley-Davidson is speaking to those of us who want personal freedom. I would imagine that's pretty much all of us, right? Notice the three movements within these six words: *We* is positioned in such a way as to communicate "we are here for you." *Fulfill dreams* is speaking to a human desire we all have. And last but not least, *personal freedom* is speaking the language of FOMO. Who doesn't want personal freedom? It's in all of us.

When you see someone riding a Harley, the company hopes you don't just see a motorcycle; they hope you see someone experiencing personal freedom, followed by, "I want to experience that too." In other words, *you can belong before you believe.* Or in this case, *you can belong before you ride.*

During

From this starting point, Harley-Davidson expands the explanation of the community it's trying to develop by adding the following description to their six-word company description:

> We fulfill dreams of personal freedom—it's our purpose, and we take it seriously. And while freedom means different things to different people, it's a bond that brings Harley-Davidson customers, employees, dealers, suppliers and enthusiasts together.[35]

They cast a wide net with their first six words, and then they bring the net in by defining the "Harley Nation"—customers, employees, dealers, suppliers, and enthusiasts. Defining your larger community is the first step in creating FOMO. Much like the University of Georgia calls their community Bulldog Nation, how would you define your community? For our church, it's Gwinnett County, Georgia. Defining the community you're trying to serve helps create specific boundaries and distinctions.

In other words, *who are you specifically FOR?*

I love how Harley-Davidson has included "suppliers" as part of their community. As a result, suppliers see themselves not just as vendors but as a part of the company. They *belong.*

So smart. So powerful.

After

This is where the magic happens. A purchase of a Harley-Davidson isn't the end; it's only the beginning. You have now taken a step closer into the belonging.

The H.O.G. membership program stands for Harley Ownership Group. There are more than 1,400 official H.O.G. chapters around the world. The program provides access to events, tours, exclusive information, roadside assistance, and much more. Most of all, it provides a communal sense of *belonging*. This is what FOR is all about.

Let's look at our two foundational questions from Harley-Davidson's perspective:

1. What do you *want* to be known FOR?
2. What *are* you known FOR?

Sure, there are lots of good answers to these questions, but ultimately they are striving to have the same answer. In Harley-Davidson's case, it's "personal freedom."

This appeal to a deeper sense of belonging humanizes the business and creates a culture that competitive pricing can't touch. Harley's competitors offer cheaper models, and customers sometimes have to wait because supply can be limited.

But this doesn't deter the Harley community because it's bigger than the bike. Even before the bike arrives, they can already experience a sense of belonging. They can belong to the community before riding the bike. In that moment, they've already experienced the thrill of personal freedom.

It's not about the bike; it's about what the bike can provide to their community. A similar example is how Frank Blake describes Home Depot. "We don't sell drill bits," Frank says. "We sell the feeling of accomplishment when the bookshelf is finished and a spouse comments on how great it looks. We're selling that feeling."

The same is true for all of us. It's not about our product; it's about the feeling or emotion that our products or services provide. It's not about the nonprofit; it's about how the nonprofit is changing people's lives for the better, and about the opportunity to belong to that kind of difference maker.

If you're a business leader, how are you leveraging the *before*, *during*, and *after* movements of the purchase? If you're a nonprofit leader, how can people belong before they believe or before they donate? How is your purpose baked into the purchase? And what feeling or emotion are you providing in the process?

When you have this kind of heart for your community, you don't have to compete on price.

Without community, you're a commodity.

HOW TO BUILD A
Digital Community

Before we go any further, I want to pause and talk to those who may think that all this sounds too far removed from the harsh real world. I get it. So let's deal with a harsh real-world example and show you the power of being FOR the community.

A common challenge for most businesses and nonprofits is how to respond to the Amazon Effect. Simply put, the Amazon Effect is the disruption of the retail space with e-commerce. And yet the impact isn't reserved just for retailers. Life in this digital age is impacting every organization.

Churches are certainly feeling it in both good and bad ways. For example, through digital *giving* options, people don't have to be at church every week to give financially, and because of digital *viewing* options, they don't have to be there in person every week. It may seem like a small thing, but attendance patterns at churches are changing. Should this be a concern? What does it mean for the future? How do we leverage the Amazon Effect instead of fight against it?

All good questions. It's why I wanted to pause before finishing the brand loyalty journey by talking about how to build a digital community. A mistake I see a lot of churches making is assuming that posting content online equals a digital strategy. It is certainly a beginning, but it is not a comprehensive digital strategy. Far from it.

The reason is that the spotlight is still on the organization: *Here's our content. Look at what we're providing.* Lots of monologue, very little dialogue.

Building a passionate digital community requires a more thoughtful, caring approach than just clicking the send button. An effective digital strategy must ask this question: How can we add value to a larger digital community, including but not exclusive to our customers? For example, talking to Home Depot customers is one thing; adding value and tips online to homeowners, regardless of where they shop, is a larger thing.

As large as your customer base is, odds are the community is larger. After all, it's a big world out there, and thanks to the internet, adding value to that larger community is a few clicks away. Technology should not isolate the community from one another. When applied correctly, technology connects and builds a community.

TECHNOLOGY should not isolate the community from one another.

That said, what does it look like to develop a strategy and build a digital community?

Building a Digital Community

From what I've observed, the best lessons on how to do this often come from the scrappy start-up world. In this chapter, you're going to be introduced to Zim Ugochukwu. I've learned a lot from studying the work of Zim, Eryn Eddy, and other entrepreneurs who started with very little and in a short amount of time built a digital community. Perhaps the most important lesson I've observed is a genuine care, respect, and love for their digital community. This creates an emotional bond that leads to a loyal following. Here's how I think they did it:

- Listen to the community.
- Talk with the community.
- Celebrate the community.

Sure, there are more than three strategies to building a digital community, and posting content is certainly one of them. However, my observation is that these three are the ones that are most often absent in digital strategies.

1. Listen to the community. Listening is quickly becoming a source of great insight for companies. If you don't have the resources of a large company, however, you can eavesdrop on your community in a cost-effective way. Simply search the hashtag of your local community and see what's happening. For example, I live in a town called Suwanee. By searching #Suwanee on Instagram, I simply get to see what kind of conversations are happening. This morning, there were lots of posts about a concert that happened in Suwanee over the weekend. People here love events. There is also a lot of diversity to be seen as I scroll through the #Suwanee feed.

Listening like this can give you tips and insights about your community. The better you know your community, the better you can serve your community.

2. *Talk with your community*. It's important to talk *with* your community more than *at* your community. A great way to do this is to ask questions. There are far too many sentences than questions in the digital space. When a brand or business asks a question, it requires listening. Here are a few questions your organization can ask:

- How's your day going?
- What's the best tip on parenting you've ever heard?
- If you could only go to one concert, what would it be?
- What's the best book you've read in the past six months?
- Who in our community deserves encouragement and recognition?
- Who was your biggest influence before you turned twenty, and why?
- What's the best vacation spot you visited in the last two years?

What may be confusing about these questions is that they have nothing to do with your business or organization.

And that's the point. We need to arrive at a place in our relationship with our community that the conversation doesn't always have to be about the business. That's part of the problem with most advertising today. There's always a hidden, or not so hidden, agenda. Are we *really* FOR the community, or are we pretending to be?

Asking questions like these puts us in a great position to interact with our community in ways that aren't directly connected to the organization. It allows us to see the community as people first and potential customers second. It humanizes the business while leveraging technology to do so. When you can leverage technology to become more personable, well, that's a beautiful, counterintuitive way to become less robotic and more human. And with all due respect to robots, the Terminator, and Google, being human will always win.

3. *Celebrate the community.* One of the best ways to build your digital community is celebrating the people in it. Remember what we said at the beginning of the book—winning brands of the future will be more concerned with becoming fans of the customer instead of trying to get the customer to become fans of the brand. This is one of the best ways to make this come to life.

Leverage social media to highlight people who are doing great things in your community. Thank a teacher, a firefighter, a businessperson, a customer, or a student as a few examples. In the bonus materials in the back of the book, we provide a link to access a Weekly Social Media Guide. This guide provides one example for each day of the week for your organization to celebrate and highlight someone in the community. For example, on Tuesday you'll highlight a local school or teacher. Some organizations wonder if this shows favoritism by only highlighting one school, but remember, you are going to follow this plan each week. You'll highlight a different school or teacher each Tuesday.

The social media guide we provide offers a plan for each day of the week. Five days a week, fifty-two weeks a year adds up to 260 celebratory moments from you to the community at large.

Trust me. Few organizations are doing this because they're too busy talking about themselves. A bank executive recently questioned this approach by saying, "I don't see other organizations doing this, so I'm not sure we need to be doing this."

"This is precisely why you need to be doing this," I replied. Ironically, this bank's marketing proudly features the word *local*. It's easy to put the word *local* in our advertising and make local media ad buys. But remember, customers are too savvy for what we say about ourselves. They are watching to see if we truly *are* local. The way we prove this is to show we actually do care. Taking a moment to structure a celebratory system on your social media feed is a simple way to show you care. Remember what Truett said: "If a person is breathing, they need encouraging."

When a business becomes a source of encouragement and support, the community no longer sees it just as a business but as a friend. And when you are FOR your community, your community will be FOR you.

As the bank executive pointed out, other organizations aren't doing this.

The door is wide open.

Influence beyond the Business

This leads us back to the final two mileposts on the brand loyalty journey.

Before we go any further, let's do a quick recap. The first step is creating a sense of *belonging*—giving people the opportunity to belong to something worthwhile. Factoring that kind of purpose into the purchase creates an emotional bond with people and allows you to build a community to belong to, not just to sell to. All of this is built on the necessity of being an authentic, credible source of influence. And this leads us to Zim's story.

Zim started and sold a travel business called Travel Noire. Her story is quite amazing. She was born in Minnesota to two

Nigerian immigrants. Prior to starting Travel Noire, she cloned a gene as a biologist, ran a national antitobacco campaign with her best friend, helped open a civil rights museum, lived in India, and traveled through 90 percent of Asia—all before she was thirty.

Suddenly I feel really old. And tired.

Zim also is an accomplished photographer. Zim learned photography while in high school. This gave her insights and an eye for great photos. When she started Travel Noire, she posted user-generated content, sourcing beautiful photos and creating her community in the process.

Let's fast-forward to selling her company, Travel Noire, to Blavity. We often want to focus on the highlight reel of entrepreneurs, asking them about the selling price and their plans for the future. All good things to ask, but we often miss the starting point.

Zim didn't start selling to customers first; Zim started building and adding value to the travel community.

Zim influenced her community first and sold to them second.

"This is where I see a lot of start-ups making mistakes," she said. "They start selling to customers without building a community first. And community often takes time to build."

In a world that wants to make a quick buck or go viral on social media, Zim provides a huge lesson for all of us: *community first; sell second.*

What Zim was doing in the early days was adding value to the travel community, no strings attached. She was FOR them. She had been to places that many only dreamed of. She became their virtual travel guide. The more she added value, the more the community was built. She became a trusted guide. And trust is invaluable in building a community like this.

We don't do business with people we don't trust. At least not for long.

This is the power of being FOR your community. When a community sees you as a trusted source, your credibility grows. This leads to a very important process.

Credibility leads to *influence*. Influence leads to *community*. Community leads to *belonging*. Belonging leads to FOMO.

See how that works?

It's important to point out that not everyone who followed Zim's advice became a customer. That's not a bad thing. It's actually a really good thing. It shows you have an authentic, credible voice of really wanting to help people. And when people see that, many of them want to help you.

CREDIBILITY leads to *influence*. Influence leads to *community*. Community leads to *belonging*. Belonging leads to *FOMO*.

It all goes back to the question, "What do you want to be known FOR?"

Here's how Zim's company Travel Noire answered it:

Travel Noire at its core is about transformation. Our brand is for people who want to unlock their potential, build meaningful relationships, and change the world. Collectively, our team (and the brilliant travelers we work with) have been to every continent on the planet. We have drawn from the breadth and depth of our experiences to design content that immerses you in the culture of a destination.[36]

As you can see, Zim built a business based on authenticity, credibility, and community. This leads us to another series of questions—*influence questions*—to ask ourselves and the organization:

- What kind of expertise do I have that I can freely share with others?
- What kind of experience do I have that would be valuable for others to learn from?
- How can our organization become a leading voice of influence in our category?

It's easy to dismiss our experience, background, and training as no big deal. We underestimate it. It's another reason that Zim's story is so helpful. She didn't overlook her travel experience. She didn't dismiss it either because it was something she enjoyed. There's a saying in the start-up world that "there are riches in the niches." Zim found a niche in the travel world and turned it into influence and eventually a business.

Where's your niche?

Impact from the Business

When the floodwaters from Hurricane Harvey eventually hit their Houston home, J. C. Spencer and his wife, Karen, realized it was time to act.

"We had to get out of there, so I called Chick-fil-A—now

that sounds kind of funny," J. C. told *Good Morning America*. "I ordered two grilled chicken burritos with extra egg and a boat."[37]

Answering the phone was restaurant manager Jeffrey Urban, who knew J. C. because he was a regular customer. "He was saying he was trying to reach out to people, and he couldn't get any response from 911," Urban told CNN. "So he called Chick-fil-A to see if we could help him out."[38]

Long, wonderful story short, another employee at the store had a boat, and within a few minutes they arrived with a boat and Jet Ski. The chicken burritos would have to wait another day.

Granted, this is quite a dramatic story, but it illustrates what Chick-fil-A wants to be known FOR—a brand that inspires people to take good care of each other.

This is impact beyond the business. It's good for goodness' sake, no strings attached. It also leads to deep customer loyalty. Sure, you can't bring a boat to everyone's house, but you can do it for one person. And do you think the Spencers are loyal customers to Chick-fil-A?

The point is that our impact must flow well beyond the walls, physical and virtual, of our business and organization. For example, churches can too often focus on what happens inside the four walls while rarely looking out into the community. It's why we must move beyond the boundaries of our organizations and interact with our communities by asking a simple but powerful question: *How can we help?*

In the early days of Gwinnett Church, before we even started meeting officially, our team met with the officials from the local government of the town we're in—Sugar Hill. We asked them this question: "How can we help?" It's easy to assume we know the answer to that. I thought I did, but I quickly discovered I was wrong. It was also an important reminder of something that's true for all of us: *the better you know the community surrounding your business, the better your business can serve the surrounding community.*

One of the best practices you can implement for your business is to ask the mayor or city officials of your community this question. Be curious. Search for problems that your business or organization can solve. It certainly doesn't obligate you in any way, but what you will find often helps both the community and the organization.

For example, when we asked the city officials of Sugar Hill, "How can we help?" I heard an answer that caught me by surprise. The answer they gave wasn't one I would have predicted.

"We have a local amphitheater that most of the community doesn't know about, and it's very nice. Could you tell your church about the amphitheater?" was their response.

I've lived in Gwinnett County most of my life, and this was news to me.

"Wait, Sugar Hill has an amphitheater?" was my response. "Where is it?"

"See," I heard back, "that's what we hear all the time."

From Sugar Hill's perspective, they had a beautiful venue few knew about, even natives like me. Now that we had this information, we were in a better position to add value to Sugar Hill, showing them we are FOR them. As the old adage says, "A problem well-defined is half-solved."

The city of Sugar Hill had defined a problem for us. During the meeting, we came up with a solution. Our church would host a concert for the community. We invited a local band to play cover songs to help kick off the summer season. It wasn't church music because the concert wasn't for us or about us. It was music for everyone because the goal was to help the community, not the church. However, by helping the community, we were helping the church, because the two can't be separated. And that's the power of being FOR the community.

One of the best things you can do for your business is to ask teachers, government leaders, customers, and friends in the community, "How can we help?"

This concert was a foundational moment in our church's culture because we hadn't even launched our permanent location in Sugar Hill. As a result, it puzzled people. "Why would you do this when there's no inherent value for the church?"

Easy answer.

Because the community told us it would help.

Gwinnett Church

Sure, you can't do everything, but you can do something. And this is something we could do.

It gave a tangible answer to the statement of what we were FOR. "What does FOR Gwinnett mean?" Well, it means a lot of things, but one example is, *we throw concerts for our city when they ask us for help.*

This concert helped set the tone for what our church was going to be about. We wanted to be a value-add from the very beginning to the community around us. We wanted to delight and surprise people from the very beginning.

The point isn't to completely avoid talking about your business or products; the point is to make sure the emphasis always comes back to *adding value* to the world around you.

It goes back to the beginning of the book when we discussed Truett's strategy: *Truett was more interested in the business growing people than he was in people growing the business. And that's exactly how his business grew.*

In today's world, customers want to do business with businesses they believe in. It's not enough to have quality service. The business must have quality people. To attract quality people, the mission of the business must be bigger than the business itself. The core of the business needs to be moving toward something—FOR something and FOR someone.

When you look at advertising and marketing through this filter, you begin to see how shallow it is when companies tell us how much better they are than their competitors. That worked yesterday. It's quite boring today. Customers are more interested in what you stand FOR than in who or what you stand against.

And why is that? It's because of this truth in the new world of business: *winning brands of today will be more interested in becoming fans of the customer instead of convincing customers to become fans of the brand.* As marketing expert Joey Reiman says, "The purpose of business is not just to create value but to add value to people's lives."[39]

The word *people* in Joey's statement is so important. He didn't say *customers*; he said *people*. This is what being FOR the community is all about—adding value online and offline to people's lives, whether or not they're customers. When a brand creates something that makes life better, people notice. They talk. They're impressed. They become a sales force for free— partly because it's a road few businesses travel on.

Want to know a secret? I think the fact that you're reading this book shows it's a road *you* want to travel on as well. And when you do, chances are you'll find Domino's Pizza has fixed a pothole or two along the way.

SECTION 4

FOR

YOU

Tim Tassopoulos is one of the nicest people I know.

He's also one of the sharpest.

Both explain his career path from working as a high school student at a local Chick-fil-A to eventually becoming president of the company.

Even though I've been gone from Chick-fil-A for quite a while now, Tim is still kind enough to have lunch with me, which reinforces the first sentence on this page.

At each lunch, I come with a series of questions for Tim, hoping to soak up as much wisdom as I can. A few years ago, I asked him a fantastic question: "What's your definition of *success?*"

Well, at least I thought it was fantastic.

"That's the wrong question," Tim said.

And before you think his response puts the first sentence on this page in jeopardy, he kept going: "Success is measuring yourself against other people. Excellence is measuring yourself against your own potential. When you choose excellence, you move closer to your potential. You've got a lot of potential, Jeff.

The question isn't about success; the question is, 'Will you move closer to your potential?'"

That question isn't just for me. The burrito at lunch was just for me, but the question Tim asked is for both of us. *Will we move closer to our potential?*

One of my hopes in writing this book is that it will help us leverage more of our potential that often lies dormant. Too often, we measure our success by comparing ourselves to other people, while rarely pausing long enough to ask ourselves a better question: "What is my potential?"

This is the question of excellence, a pathway to harvesting more of our potential that will result in greater impact for others. I believe there is enormous, untapped potential in businesses and nonprofits. But ultimately organizations don't move toward potential; people do. When enough people move closer to their potential, the momentum it will generate will move the business forward.

It's why, before concluding the book, we have one final place we need to go.

It's not enough to be FOR the customer, team, and community. You have to understand how to be FOR you—to grow and move closer to your own potential.

As Truett was fond of saying, "If it is to be, it is up to me."

Remain **INSPIRED**

CHAPTER 18

I f we're going to move anywhere close to our potential, we're going to have to remain inspired.

Think about it. Nothing significant is created, transformed, or turned around without inspiration. The reason many companies have lost their way is that inspiration walked out the door a long time ago. The reason many marriages lost their way is that it was assumed inspiration would automatically stick around. The reason many people have lost their way is that they stopped looking forward.

We assumed something wrong about inspiration. We assumed if we had to fight for it, then it must not be real. We assumed it was enough to go to a conference once a year. We assumed there were more important things to do than remaining inspired.

We assumed inspiration rarely showed up on the bottom line.

Ironically, thriving companies are inspired companies. You feel it. You sense it. You experience it. It takes inspiration for a company to say, "It's not enough to be the best company *in* the world; we must be the best company *FOR* the world."

We need more organizational cultures like that. We need more inspired businesses. We need more inspired churches. We need more inspired nonprofits. We need more inspired schools.

For this to happen, we're going to need more inspired people.

I've discovered something about inspiration though. It's not enough to be inspired; you must remain inspired.

We have to fight for it. It's like Batman in the *Dark Knight Trilogy*. One minute, Commissioner Gordon is talking to Batman—then poof! He turns around, and Batman is gone.

Inspiration often goes poof. It seems fickle. One minute it likes you; the next minute it's gone. There's a reason for this. Inspiration has an enemy. It's called "everyday life."

Everyday life is rough on inspiration. It's why 363 days of everyday life are more powerful than two days at a conference. In fact, does the following sound a little familiar?

The conference notebook is full of ideas.

Each speaker seemed to be having a personal conversation with me. How did she know this was exactly what I needed to hear, both personally and professionally?

The team is going to love this. It's the change we need to take it to the next level. It's the change I need to take it to the next level.

The agenda for our next meeting is downloading what I learned at the conference. I have my notebook by my side and start reading through all my highlights. I glance up occasionally, and the inspiration I thought it would create seems to only produce some quizzical looks, eventually followed by skeptical questions. "But how would that work here?" "That sounds great, but how can we do that with all the work already happening here?"

Slowly the inspiration from the conference fades away. It lasted all of four days.

I have a hunch this fictional account happens every week in organizations around the world. The greatest danger isn't just to the organization though. The greatest danger is what it can potentially do to you.

We need an inspired you.

One of the best ways you can be FOR the customer, the team, and the community is giving them an inspired, healthy you. It's what this section is about, and in many ways, it's the most important part of the book. Like anything, life flows from a source. The life of an organization, or lack thereof, flows from the people of the organization.

It's impossible to have a healthy organization with unhealthy people.

And eventually an unhealthy organization can be turned around with healthy people. The question is, "What kind of life is flowing from you and me?"

In this section, we are going to talk about your personal brand. Think of it as "You, Inc." Just like an organization has a brand, individuals have a brand too. The idea of a personal brand may be a bit uncomfortable, but it can dictate whether or not we reach our potential.

The reality for all of us is that we have an emotional climate that follows us. When we walk into a room, the climate of our brand comes with us. There are all sorts of climates—cold climates, warm climates, hot climates.

Climates are important. They help dictate the forecast. It's why a blizzard won't happen near Maui. It's why you don't wear shorts to a Green Bay Packers game in January.

It's not just true with the weather. The relational climate in your organization dictates the forecast of your organization. And it's not just true with organizations; it's true with you and me.

Our personal climates dictate the forecast of our relationships, both personally and professionally. Years ago, I did a sermon series called "Climate Change." Our media team created a video about this concept showing people in a meeting at work. Above their heads, they had placed weather symbols letting everyone in the room know what their emotional climate was that day. Over one person's head was a storm cloud. Everyone knew to stay away from that person. The biggest problem, though, was that the person with the storm cloud over their head couldn't see it. They couldn't see how the storm cloud was affecting their relationships. They couldn't see how the storm cloud was affecting them personally. Sadly, we are often our own worst enemy.

It's why we need to talk about our climate and personal brand. We're not just going to talk about this though. In the bonus section of the book, you'll have an opportunity to take a personal brand assessment. This will help you understand what your personal brand is and how you can improve it. The good news for each of us is we don't have to live our lives trapped under a cloud. We can carry a climate into our lives that helps others and ourselves. It will take work, but the reward is invaluable. The personal brand assessment can help with this.

Now, if you're perfect and have no issues, you have my permission to stop reading. For the rest of us, let's keep moving forward.

Before we get to the assessment, we need to revisit the two questions this book is built around and ask them from a slightly different perspective.

You, Inc.

If you were a corporation, we would begin with the two FOR questions:

- What do *you* want to be known FOR?
- What are *you* known FOR?

One of the reasons many people feel a disconnect at work and in their personal life is that the answers to these two questions are different. When people say they feel a lack of purpose at work, it's often because the purpose at work is unknown or inconsistent with their personal purpose.

More often than that is the reality that many people haven't done the introspective work of asking themselves these two questions. So let's start here: *What do you want to be known FOR?*

I'll admit. It's an intimidating question, so let's learn once again from Truett Cathy.

His life verse from the Bible answered this question for him. Proverbs 22:1 (ESV) reads, "A good name is to be chosen rather than great riches."

Regardless of your perspective on the Bible, this is a fantastic answer to the question, "What do you want to be known FOR?" It's also important to note that this verse is a great answer to the question, "What is branding?" When a company makes decisions through the filter of wanting a good name, the long-term value of the brand name increases.

Closed on Sundays

An example of this is Truett's decision to close his restaurant on Sundays. People often point to how much money Chick-fil-A "loses" by being closed one day a week. This was perhaps an even more difficult decision when Chick-fil-A was exclusively in shopping malls. Sunday was a huge day for malls, and there Chick-fil-A sat, closed up and shut down.

Looking back on the early days, Truett admitted that closing down one day a week was as much from exhaustion as it was from inspiration. But as the business grew, the Sunday question loomed large. As he signed agreements with shopping malls, the perplexed looks on the other side of the table told him all he needed to know. "Why are you closed on one of the busiest days of the week?" As the company grew, the whispers grew louder. "Eventually he'll change his mind. No one will walk away from that much money just for a principle."

Decisions and moments like these eventually land before all of us. Will we stay true to who we want to be and what we want to be known FOR, or will we make subtle compromises along the way? Long-term gain versus short-term gain. It's a conundrum as old as time.

For Truett, it was a simple decision. Of the ten commandments given to the Israelites in the Old Testament, commandment #4 reads, "Remember the Sabbath day, to keep it holy. Six days you shall labor, and do all your work, but the seventh day is a Sabbath to the LORD your God" (Exodus 20:8–10 ESV).

The word *Sabbath* refers to "a day of religious observance and abstinence from work." So on Saturday night, Truett turned off the lights and locked the doors and didn't return until early Monday morning.

Why? It's simple.

"A good name is to be chosen rather than great riches."

When you answer the question of what you want to be known FOR in this way, it guides your decision making. You actually sleep better at night. The stock market can take away financial gains, but it can't take away your character and integrity—unless you give it the opportunity.

Practically speaking, what does this look like on an everyday basis? It may make us uncomfortable to talk about our personal brand, but in essence that's what a good name means. In other words, to ask how you can improve your "good name" is another way to ask how you can improve your "personal brand." But as we're about to see, this isn't ultimately about you. It's actually a great way to be FOR the customer, team, and community. For this to happen, we're going to need a healthy and inspired you—clear on your purpose, locked in on purpose, remaining inspired.

To arrive there, I want to give you seven of the best tips I know of to enhance your personal brand. The overarching principle to do this is to *remain inspired*. These seven practical tips will help you give *the best you* to the world around you.

And again, that's one of the best ways to show you're FOR them.

SEVEN WAYS TO
Improve You, Inc.

CHAPTER 19

1. Your Life Moves to a Better Place When You Move at a Sustainable Pace

Fatigue makes cowards of us all," the legendary football coach Vince Lombardi taught his team.[40] It also makes bad decisions, is cranky, and chooses short-term over long-term almost every time.

One of the reasons we lose our inspiration is that we're just tired. Exhausted actually. There is nothing to give. It's hard to be FOR others when the well is dry in us.

I understand. I'm writing this in a season where my pace is challenging. I have this book deadline in front of me. I start a new sermon series at Gwinnett Church this coming Sunday. We're opening up our second Gwinnett Church location. I want to do all of it really well. More importantly, I also want to be a great husband and dad, get plenty of exercise, etc. I'm not complaining about any of this. You have your own list.

My point is I can trick myself into thinking I can do what's ahead of me while running on fumes. Sure, there are seasons that are busier than others. This is one of those for me. But rest cannot be an option. It's a necessity. What I've discovered about my health is that if I won't slow down, my body will slow me down. It usually starts with a sore throat, and the next thing I know, I'm sick at home. It took me years to figure this out. Rather than fight against rest, I try to cooperate with the gift of rest.

For some of us, rest seems weak. *I can power through*, we tell ourselves. Here's the problem with that. Have you ever been working on a problem at work and decided to take a break? Maybe you go for a walk outside, come back in, and then instantly see the solution? What just happened?

You experienced the power of rest. Your mind rested and saw the solution.

Rest isn't for the weak; rest is for the wise.

If we don't see that, our kids do. In his book *Find Your Strongest Life*, Marcus Buckingham pointed out a study of one thousand young people in the third through twelfth grades. They were asked one question: "If you were granted one wish that would change the way that your mother's/your father's work affects your life, what would that wish be?"[41]

More than six hundred mothers and fathers were asked to guess what they thought the answer would be. Most of them said their children would wish for more time with them. They were wrong. Only 10 percent said that about their moms, and only 15.5 percent said that about their dads. If they didn't want more time, what did they want? Most of the children wished their parents would be *less stressed and tired*. Those kids are smart. It makes sense. Being less stressed and tired would help us be better parents. It would help us be better humans too.

Specifically, here are three small ways to achieve a better pace. One is for a day, the second for a week, and the third for a quarter.

One extra hour of sleep. This week increase the number of hours of sleep you get by one hour a night. Just try it and see what happens.

Fasting. Try going twenty-four hours without social media and email. I know, I know—it may feel like it's impossible for you. How about just trying it? If you can't do email, try social media. Try a social media and email fast for one whole day.

Quarterly recharge. Try to build in a getaway or reflection day each quarter. The goal of that day is exercise, solitude, reading, reflecting on the last quarter, and looking ahead to the next quarter. Recharging takes time. A full day of recharge is a great way to do that. A slow, consistent charge is the best way to bring a battery back to life. The same is true for you.

It's not about working less; it's about working smart.

Whenever I talk about this in the business world, people look at me like I've either lost my mind or I don't know what it's like out there in the real world. That's when I ask them if they've ever helped win a world war. Usually the answer is no—and by usually I mean *always*. The answer is no—always.

Then I point to Winston Churchill, the British prime minister who helped win World War II against unbelievable odds. He was famous for his speeches, his courage, and his wit. He was also famous for taking an afternoon nap—every single day. With all due respect to you and me, Winston Churchill had a few more challenging things on his to-do list. He knew a rested Winston was one of the best gifts he could give his nation, his troops, and the world.

The same is true for you. Your life moves to a better place when you move at a sustainable pace. You can leverage this principle or rail against it.

A good name requires rest. Remaining inspired does too.

2. Think 30

When asked by a reporter what was wrong with most people in his day, the famous Nobel prize winner Dr. Albert Schweitzer said, "Men simply don't think."[42]

Thinking more is the key to more. It's not enough to say you need to think more. We need a plan.

THINKING *more* **is the key to more.**

Several years ago, I came up with a personal challenge called Think 30. The challenge was to think for thirty minutes a day. It could be about something at work or something personal; sometimes I just stared at a blank page. Some days were frustrating. But sometimes it happened. I got an idea I never would have gotten otherwise. I never knew when it would happen, and that's the point. Thinking is like fishing. Some days are better than others, but you never catch something unless you show up.

What does a Think 30 day look like? Good question. I've discovered it's usually better when I'm rested. (See point #1.) For me, I do my best thinking in the morning. Once you've carved out the time, here's how to leverage thirty minutes of thinking:

- Before you start, read something for at least five minutes. It may be a meditation or the current book you're reading—anything to get your mind going in the right direction.

- Set a timer for ten minutes. This will help you avoid the urge to check your phone, email, Facebook, and the like. The hardest ten minutes of the Think 30 is the first ten because your brain is screaming to do something else. The brain tries to conserve energy, and thinking expends a lot of energy. No wonder we end up watching cat videos on YouTube when we try to think. Don't let your brain trick you. Trick your brain instead with three ten-minute increments.

- Write at the top of the page the goal for this particular Think 30 session. It may be thinking about a problem at work that needs a solution, planning out your dream vacation, pondering how to increase your income or how to be a better spouse, etc. My experience is that it's usually better to have a specific goal, although there are times when I just sit down with a blank page and a cup of coffee and see what happens.

- Once your first ten-minute session is over, set your timer for the second ten-minute session. During this time, write down any thought that comes to mind. Even if you can't think of anything to write down, just write, "I can't think of anything to write down." The goal here is quantity, not quality. At the end of the ten minutes, put your pen down and go on to the last ten-minute session.

- In this ten-minute session, you look for connections in what you just wrote down. Is there a sentence, phrase, or word that connects and can be built on? Steve Jobs said, "Creativity is just connecting things."[43] In this final ten-minute session, you're becoming more creative by simply making connections with what you just thought about and wrote down.

And that's it. Thirty minutes a day. As I mentioned earlier, some days you get nothing; some days you get gold. You just never know unless you show up. What I'm convinced of is this: if you think more, you'll accomplish more.

3. A Great Day Begins the Night Before

It sounds simple, but one of the best ways to remain inspired is to have more great days. If only life was that simple, right?

However, the principle that *a great day begins the night before* helps improve the odds of having more days like this.

One of the best ways to have a great day is to define the day before what that would look like. Before going to bed, write down three simple wins that would need to take place for tomorrow to be a great day. It doesn't have to be huge; it just needs to be three wins that will help guide you in the morning. This way, you've already set a path when your feet hit the ground. If you don't do this, urgency does it for you—and as we all know, the urgent screams to be the most important.

4. How to Find a Mentor

Iron sharpens iron. This timeless principle is one of the best ways to remain inspired and build your good name. Surrounding yourself with people who will sharpen, challenge, and inspire you is one of the best things you can do FOR you. Of course, this isn't as easy as it sounds. "Where do you find the iron, the sharpeners, the mentors?" It's a question I hear a lot.

One of the best ways to find a mentor is to be clear on who you are looking for, and this goes back to being clear about who you are wanting to become. The more you define who you want to be, the more you define who you want your mentor to be.

Who do you look up to? Who do you admire? What qualities are there that you want to emulate? It's not enough to ask someone to mentor us; we have to be clear about what we want them to do and how we think they can help us grow.

Once you've defined who you're looking for, there are two types of mentoring to leverage.

Distance mentoring. Some of the best mentors in my life are people who have never met me. Mentoring in real time and in person is great, but it doesn't have to be limited to that. This is why reading is so important. It allows you to be mentored by the very people you admire from a distance. It's why Truett Cathy said, "The two ways a person improves is the books they read and the people they interact with."

Real-time mentoring. One of the best ways to determine who should be a sharpener in your life is to look around and ask, "Which of the people I admire is further along in life than me?" This doesn't have to be limited to business. For example, when Wendy and I were expecting our first child, I made a list of men with teenage or young adult children whom I respected and admired. I asked if I could take them to breakfast and learn from them as dads. They sharpened me as a father, and I still implement the advice I heard from them to this day. In fact, now that my kids are teenagers, I'm sharing that invaluable advice with younger dads.

5. Ask Big

When our kids were young, we were big fans of Pixar movies like *Finding Nemo*. I quickly became a fan of the organization when I saw a behind-the-scenes video of their corporate headquarters. Fast-forward to our daughter's senior year of high school. We wanted to take her on a trip to celebrate, and she decided on visiting California. That's when I thought of the idea of writing Pixar a letter and asking them if we could tour their offices. *How cool would that be?*

So, long story short, I sent a handwritten note to Pixar, explaining what I wanted to do and asking if they could help create a lasting memory for our family as we celebrated my daughter's graduation. "Would it be possible to get a personal tour of the Pixar headquarters?" As I wrote the note, I bounced back and forth between the emotions of "this is a waste of time and a good postage stamp because they'll never respond" to "how amazing would this be!"

I kept on writing and eventually mailed the letter because I've realized something about asking big. My responsibility is not the answer; my responsibility is *the ask*. I should never stop asking big because I presuppose how someone will answer. My responsibility is to *ask big*. I need to be faithful to the ask and see what happens.

The very worst thing that can happen is they say no. Or, as happens many times, you just never hear back. That's okay. Keep asking. Because there are times when you *do* get a response back. And asking big is a sign that you are remaining inspired. Yes, you will receive more noes than yeses. But the point is to keep asking, keep dreaming, keep believing. Remain inspired.

Imagine my surprise when five months after writing the letter to Pixar, I got a phone call from a number in Oakland, California. My first thought was, *I don't know anyone from Oakland, California.* I hit decline on my phone and moved on. I discovered later that I had a voice mail from a phone number in California. "Mr. Henderson, this is Wendy from Pixar. We received your note, and we'd love to give you and your family a tour . . ."

I just stared at the phone in disbelief. A few weeks later, our family was getting our picture taken at the Steve Jobs Building at Pixar, Inc. During the tour, my daughter, Jesse, whispered to me, "Dad, this is so cool." I'll never forget that moment—not only because of the memory with my family but because of the lesson it reinforced in me. The entire tour I just kept thinking, *What if I had not asked big?*

When is the last time *you* asked big?

6. Find Your Voice

It's been said there are two great fears in life: death and public speaking. I understand. And yet the reality is that most great things in history (and bad things too) have happened when someone got up to speak and rallied people around their idea. For this to happen in your organization and mine, we need to find our voice and become better communicators.

Sometimes when I speak to business groups, I ask them to raise their hand if they've ever heard a boring business presentation. Everyone laughs and raises their hands. Then I ask how many of us think we might have been the reason someone raised their hand. Public speaking certainly can be daunting, but it's inevitable in any organization. This isn't limited to speaking on a platform. I define public speaking as any form of communication where you are communicating an idea or information to another human being. When people tell me they aren't a public speaker, I ask if they ever speak in meetings. The answer is, of course, yes. Then I congratulate them. They have spoken in a public setting. You are now officially a public speaker. This is why leadership and communication go hand in hand.

Eventually leadership comes with a microphone. Literally or figuratively, we are handed a microphone and asked to lead. It could be our family, a friendship, a company, a team, a homeowners association (God be with you), a school, a volunteer group, and on and on. *How* we communicate is as important as *what* we communicate. This is true whether we are in front of five people or five hundred.

One of the reasons people struggle with this is that they

haven't found their voice. For several years now, I've coached business leaders and pastors on their presentations. During this time, I've observed there are four presenter voices and we usually have one of these as a primary voice.

Those voices are the teacher, the motivator, the storyteller, and the visionary. The following chart details each of these, and the bonus section in the back of the book provides a link to an online test you can take to help you determine your primary voice.

THE TEACHER

- The voice of the teacher is instructional, with explanation as the goal.
- The weakness of this voice can potentially be a lack of connection with the crowd.
- The question the teacher must answer for the audience is, "Why is this content important?"

THE MOTIVATOR

- The voice of the motivator is action-oriented, with personal change as the goal.
- The weakness of this voice is that it can lean more on inspiration and less on content and clarity.
- The question the motivator must answer for the audience is, "What do I want you to do with this information?"

THE STORYTELLER

- The voice of the storyteller is engaging, with an emotional connection with the crowd as the goal.
- The weakness of this voice can be a lack of direction and clarity regarding the purpose of the presentation.
- The question the storyteller must answer is, "Where am I taking the audience?"

THE VISIONARY

- The voice of the visionary is inspiring, with organizational/world change as the goal.
- The weakness of this voice is clearly articulating the how behind the why of the change.
- The question the visionary must answer is, "How are we going to accomplish this?"

7. Be Humble or Be Humbled

If there is one lesson history proves over and over and over again, it's this one: be humble or be humbled. As my friend John Woodall says, "God resists the proud, and so do we."

One of my favorite books in recent years has been *Ego Is the Enemy* by Ryan Holiday. Ryan takes this teaching so seriously that he tattooed the title of his book on his right forearm as a constant reminder: "Ego is the enemy." It's a great reminder, whether you do the tattoo thing or not.

Ryan writes about the danger of having pride as a translator

227

in our life. Pride "creates a sort of myopic, onanistic obsession that warps perspective, reality, truth, and the world around us," he writes. "Receive feedback, maintain hunger, and chart a proper course in life. Pride dulls these senses. Or in other cases, it tunes up other negative parts of ourselves: sensitivity, a persecution complex, the ability to make everything about *us*."[44]

Similarly, my friend John Woodall talks about taking the low place—a concept based on a story Jesus told about the danger of going to a dinner party and sitting at the place of honor. It's a great story. You can read it in full at bible.com (search Luke 14:8–11). The point is to consistently search out the low place and go there. "For all those who exalt themselves will be humbled, and those who humble themselves will be exalted" (Luke 14:11).

Be humble or be humbled.

I experienced this my second year while working at Chick-fil-A. One of my responsibilities was serving the Denver, Colorado, market. At the time, we were opening Denver's first freestanding Chick-fil-A, and I was on the way there for the grand opening. I was flying with Bubba Cathy, Truett's son and a vice president with the company. As we approached the ticket counter, the Delta agent recognized Bubba. Chick-fil-A spends a lot of money with Delta, and the agent did a smart thing. She instantly upgraded Bubba to first-class. "Mr. Cathy," she said, "thank you for all you and your company do for Delta. I've upgraded you to first-class."

Bubba smiled, thanked her, and then said, "Could you do me another favor, please?" "Sure," she replied. Bubba turned to me. "This is my friend Jeff," he said. "I'm so grateful you upgraded me, but is there any way you can give my first-class seat to him and I'll take his seat?"

228

You could tell by the look on the face of the Delta agent that this had never happened before, dating all the way back to the days of the Wright Brothers. *No one* gives up their first-class seat. After pausing for a moment, she made the change and handed me my first-class ticket.

I had never flown first-class before. Y'all, it's awesome up there! They start off with these hot towels, an appetizer, plenty of legroom . . .

Okay, I digress. Here's my point. Would it have been wrong for Bubba to accept the first-class ticket? Not at all. If he had, would I be talking about that moment almost twenty years later? Not at all.

Instead, that moment has stayed with me. I've told thousands of people about it, and that now includes you. As a result of Bubba's taking the low place, he has been exalted numerous times because I've told that story over and over. "For all those who exalt themselves will be humbled, and those who humble themselves will be exalted." It doesn't matter what you believe about the Bible or faith; this is a life principle for all of us.

Bubba's example set a standard for me. It has now set a standard for you.

And in that moment, Bubba was practicing what he learned from his dad: "A good name is to be chosen rather than great riches."

A Bonus Question

At some point in our lives, we find ourselves at a crossroads, like Bob Dalton did. He was looking for work. He had an idea. He was afraid it wouldn't work. Ever been there?

To make things even more challenging for Bob, his mom lived on the other side of the country and was currently homeless. Sitting in his car one day, he came back to an idea he had been thinking of for a while. He wanted to create a company that provides high-quality blankets for the homeless—a "buy one, give one" approach. For every blanket sold, Bob would donate a blanket to a local homeless shelter.

Though he had been thinking about this idea for a while, he hadn't taken any action. "Oh, and the other thing," Bob adds. "I didn't know how to sew. I didn't know how to make a blanket."

In other words, there were plenty of reasons for Bob to remain seated. Inactive. Stalled.

We've all been there. Maybe you're there now. In moments like these, I believe God nudges us to take a step, to get moving. Often that's all we need. Just a step in the right direction. Maybe that's what's happening for you right now.

It's what happened to Bob. Sitting in his car that

day, he got a nudge. It was right there on the sleeve of his coffee cup. This is the actual photo from that moment.

God nudged Bob. Bob got moving. He drove to JOANN Fabrics and Crafts and bought a roll of fabric. Since he didn't know how to sew, he hired seamstresses to make blankets. He approached two hundred stores asking them to sell his blankets. Remember, *ask big*. Out of two hundred stores, 180 said no—but twenty said yes. And his company, Sackcloth and Ashes, was born.

Four and a half years later, they are well on their way to providing one million blankets to homeless shelters. And it all started with a great question: "What are you waiting for?"

Perhaps the nudge Bob received that day isn't reserved for him. Maybe this very moment is the reason you've read this book.

Perhaps you already know personally the answers to these two questions:

- What do you want to be known FOR?
- What *are* you known FOR?

But perhaps you're still nervous. Maybe like Bob, you need a bonus question, a nudge, more for your heart than for your head. After all, that's usually what overrides our fears.

Yes, it will require courage. Yes, it's scary. But no, it's not a leap. It's just a step; it's just a question. But it may be your future.

What are you waiting FOR?

Truett Cathy passed away in November 2014. Wendy and I attended his memorial service, along with thousands of other people. Much was said, and rightly so, about how he lived true to what he wanted to be known for—Proverbs 22:1. And yet it's interesting to point out that "a good name is to be chosen rather than great riches" is only half of the verse. There's a second half to the verse that, I believe, is just as important: "and favor is better than silver or gold" (ESV).

This word *favor* is an interesting choice. As I mentioned previously, one of my favorite definitions of the word FOR is "to be in favor of." To be in favor of people, to be in favor of adding value instead of extracting value, to lean more toward being the best company FOR the world, to talk more about the customer than you do your company—this is far better than silver or gold. But don't miss the subtle point here. It's not an either-or proposition.

As in Truett's case, to be in favor of people and God actually led to people and God returning the favor. I believe God blessed Truett; his wife, Jeannette; his kids; and the business. I believe people blessed Truett with their support of his business and his charities. "To be in favor of" is so powerful that sometimes not even death has the final say.

Shortly after Truett's passing, the corporate staff received a note from him thanking them for all they had done. Even now, Truett was treating the staff as family.

In the opening section of the book, we uncovered one of Truett Cathy's secrets to growing the business: *Truett was more interested in the business growing people than he was in people growing the business. And that's exactly how his business grew.*

It wasn't just true during his lifetime; it's true even now.

You and I may never have the financial resources Truett had, but he left behind an example to follow—to be more FOR others than we are FOR ourselves. In an often hypercritical and cynical world, let's be known more for who and what we're FOR than who and what we're against. It's a simple but powerful way to improve the world.

It's why these two questions will not only grow your business but also change your life. When you get crystal clear on what you want to be known for personally, life becomes an opportunity to live out that answer. So for one last time, let me ask you these two questions:

- What do you want to be known FOR?
- What *are* you known FOR?

The future is a blank page where you get to write your answer.

Write it well.

AFTERWORD

In 2000, our church decided to expand by building additional campuses rather than continuing to build on our original site. Other large churches were adopting a multisite approach as well. Where we parted ways with the conventional wisdom at the time was around branding. Rather than brand our additional sites in a way that would associate them with our original campus, we decided that each new campus would be branded to reflect the community it served. When we built in the business district of Buckhead, we named the church Buckhead Church. When we built in the city of Woodstock, we named the church Woodstock City Church.

As Jeff Henderson describes in chapter 2, when we decided to expand to the east, I asked him to step down from his role as lead pastor of Buckhead Church and launch a new church in Gwinnett County. What he didn't tell you is that starting a church from scratch is a lot . . . as in a *whole* lot . . . of hard work. Another detail he brushed by quickly is that he had already done that once. And once is enough for anyone. Jeff left an extraordinarily successful, strategically positioned church that he had been instrumental in launching a few years earlier. Just when things were going well, I asked him to pick up and leave to do it all again. To start over—as in no building, no land, no office, and a big question mark about how many people would choose to join Jeff and his family to participate in this start-up.

As you picked up from the chapters that follow, this grand experiment worked—in large part because of the principles Jeff shares in this book. I may be Jeff's current boss, but I promise you I've learned as much from him as he has from me. Truth is, everyone on our six-hundred-person staff has been directly or indirectly impacted by Jeff's leadership, creativity, and unrelenting passion to communicate that we are genuinely FOR people.

And that brings me to the one other facet of Jeff's church-planting experience that I feel compelled to share, because it underscores so much of what Jeff shares in this fabulous book. He touched on it, but I want to tell it from my perspective and the perspective of our staff who watched from the sidelines as Jeff and his team prepared to launch Gwinnett Church.

As I mentioned, we were choosing names for our sites that identified them with the communities they served. So one of the first decisions Jeff and his team had to make was the name for this new church. Gwinnett County contains several cities and regions that are well-known both inside and outside the county. But instead of choosing a city or even a region in the county, Jeff announced to our management team that he wanted to brand the church to the *entire* county. He wanted to name it Gwinnett Church.

If I remember correctly, we all just stared at him. Name a church after an entire county? First, that's not how *we* do it. Second, that's not how *anybody* does it. But that's what Jeff did. As he has done on many occasions, he stretched our thinking and our vision. Names are important; church names are really important. The name of a church communicates who a church is FOR. And Jeff wasn't FOR *part* of the county; he was FOR the *entire* county. So he suggested a name that fit his vision. And that would prove to be a strategic, paradigm-shifting decision.

It took about a year to secure a site for Gwinnett Church. By then, we had all become used to the idea of a church named for a county. We were even starting to wonder if maybe we should rename some of our existing churches for the counties they were in. Clearly we weren't thinking big enough. So you can imagine our shock when Jeff dropped the next bomb. He shared this with you as well. Jeff didn't want a "Coming Soon" sign on the property; he wanted to erect a sign that didn't even include the name of the church.

We were so confused. But Jeff wasn't.

Jeff strategically chose not to advertise the *name* of the church, but rather the *vision* behind the name. For Gwinnett. The For Gwinnett campaign caught on immediately and continues to have momentum to this day. It's not only impacting the folks in Gwinnett County; it's impacting all our churches and churches around the country as more and more leaders begin to understand the power of FOR.

I want to swing back around to this portion of Jeff's story because to me it encapsulates so much of what you've just read. I often tell leaders, "Marry your mission; date your model." As Jeff has reiterated throughout *Know What You're FOR*, when you are genuinely FOR the people you serve, what you're FOR will determine what you do going forward.

ACKNOWLEDGMENTS

As I neared the finish line of writing this book, I received an email from the team at HarperCollins confirming the official publication date—October 1. I stared at that email for quite a while. October 1 was my dad's birthday. He passed away in 2013, and I miss him every day. I believe there are moments when God comforts us with an arm around the shoulder and a whisper, "Death doesn't have the final say." I'm grateful for the legacy of an amazing earthly father and the promise and presence of a wonderful heavenly Father.

And then there's my incredible mom. I could say so much about her, but instead I'll just ask you to go online and search "eighty-nine-year-old grandmother meets Tim Tebow" and you'll see for yourself. Twenty-two years ago, I was blessed with two other parents, Peggy and Everett Major. You two are personally changing the brand of "in-laws" for the better.

Thank you to the wonderful people of Gwinnett Church and Buckhead Church for giving me the honor of being your lead pastor. I will always treasure these memories. To Kristen Franklin and Lauren Espy, thank you for choosing to be a vital part of both journeys. I'm not a good enough writer to express my appreciation. To the Gwinnett Church leadership team and staff, thank you for modeling FOR for countless other churches. You inspire me.

Almost seventeen years ago, I received an email from my friend John Woodall that said, "Come work for us at North Point Ministries." He had no idea what the Lord was already doing in my heart and Wendy's. After conversations with John, Sean Seay, and Bill Willits, we made the leap. I'm grateful for their belief in me. Over these years, I have been given a front row seat to watch authentic, visionary, and excellent leadership. Thank you, Andy Stanley, Lane Jones, Rick Holliday, and North Point Ministries for that gift which blessed both my family and me.

Wendy often teases me that I've never really left Chick-fil-A. But you never really leave family, right? To Dan, Bubba, Trudy, and the entire Cathy family, I hope this book honors your deep influence on me. To David "Tribe Up" Salyers (championtribes. com), Steve Robinson, Tim Tassopoulos, Woody Faulk, Jon Bridges, Cliff Robinson, Mark Miller, Carol Thomas, Robert McLaughlin, Brad Williams, Sandy Causey, Danna Wright, and the entire Chick-fil-A team, a hearty and grateful "Eat Mor Chikin" to you all.

To David Farmer and Shane Benson, our twenty-year friendship is one of the best treasures I've found. To Kevin Jennings, thanks for helping the four of us launch LaunchYouniversity. com, even though I still struggle to set up the podcast equipment.

The greatest appreciation I can express to my friend Troy Fountain and his help with The For Company is to say, "Roll Tide." (I still can't believe I put those two words in this book.)

To my friend Carey Nieuwhof, who will soon own the internet with his leadership podcast, our conversation in Canada in the fall of 2015 is still paying dividends in my life today. Thank you. And speaking of leadership, to the leadership guru who has literally influenced millions, Dr. John Maxwell, thank you for believing in me and this message. I'm still stunned and forever grateful you would lend your name to this project. Mark Cole, you are an encourager who breathes life into people and pushes them forward. I say that from personal experience. To Lysa TerKeurst, Shae Tate, and the team from Compel, thank you for your early belief in this book and for shaping it for the better.

A quick shout-out to four business heroes. To Cheryl Bachelder, how you led the turnaround story at Popeyes Louisiana Kitchen is my all-time favorite. To Sid Mashburn, you are my fashion hero (followed closely by Farmer), and I love the hopefulness and helpfulness your business provides. Jeni Britton Bauer—you don't know me, but I love Jeni's Splendid Ice Cream. Here's hoping someone you know places this book in your hand so that my family and I can have an ice cream meeting with you someday. To my late mentor Steve Polk, I hope I'm doing a good job of stewarding your influence on me. I still miss you.

To the amazing team at Zondervan and HarperCollins, thank you for taking a chance on this rookie author. To my editor Andy Rogers, thank you for your wise counsel and fun text messages. May the Detroit Tigers and the Atlanta Braves make it to the World Series next season in your honor. There's always next season, right?

To Brandon Henderson, I'm sure two marketing guys named Henderson have to be related somewhere down the line. Thank you for working so hard to get this message into the world. David

Morris, Tom Dean, Robin Barnett, Dirk Buursma, Andrea Pancoast, and team, thank you for being FOR me. I wouldn't have met any of you without the life force known as Esther Fedorkevich. Thank you, Esther, Jill Welborn, and the entire Fedd Agency team. You're the best.

And thank you to *you*. I'm grateful you made it this far into the book. Text me your favorite takeaway or a question about what you've read. I'll text back. I promise. Here's my cell: 404-317-3946.

Finally, when I was ten, I prayed about the wife I wanted to someday marry and described her to my friend Billy Ford. That may sound crazy, but it's true. Just ask Billy. Twenty years later, God answered that prayer with Wendy Major. I love you, Wendy Jo. I'm immensely proud to be known as Wendy's husband. And I also love being known as Jesse's and Cole's dad. Even though Cole is spreading a rumor to our friends that he's working on a book called *Against*, the two of you are a gift to this world. I love seeing how you show your world God is FOR them by how well you SERVE them.

Now let's all go out and show someone we're FOR them today.

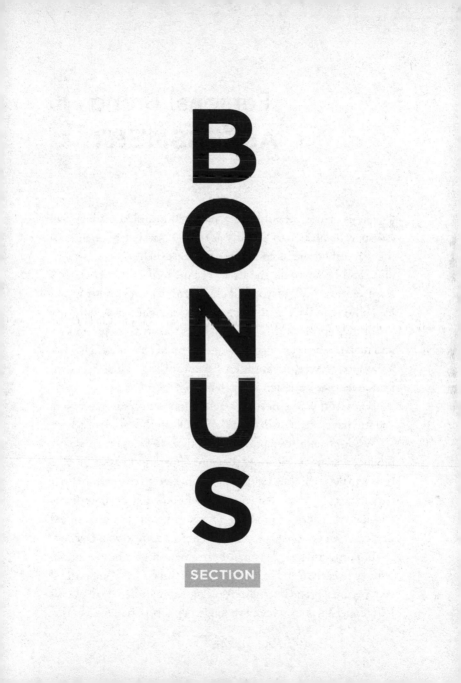

BONUS

SECTION

Personal Brand
ASSESSMENT

Like it or not, we all have a personal brand. This may feel superficial, but the reality is that, consciously or unconsciously, others assess your appearance, speech, energy, personality, and behavior all the time. From those assessments, they form opinions about your likely strengths, weaknesses, and capabilities and decide if they want to further engage with you.

Brands are helpful. They enable us to sort through options and make associations. A brand is a form of a promise. It's what a product, service, organization, event, or individual is known FOR, whether by design or by default.

So even if you've never thought about your personal brand, you still have one. It's what you stand FOR in the minds of others.

While you are attempting to get others to focus on an idea or product you are advocating, they are often still focused on you, trying to decide if they want to be connected to you personally. If they have concerns about you, they will probably never seriously consider your idea or product. That's why your personal brand matters. Your personal brand is often the gateway to your business.

Building a strong personal brand requires brand intention, brand perception, and brand calibration. One way to understand your personal brand is to take a quick assessment. To do that, visit JeffHenderson.com, where I've loaded up lots of free resources.

Find Your Voice
ASSESSMENT

As I said in section 4, leadership eventually comes with a microphone. One of the best ways to become a better communicator is to discover which of the four presenter voices are your strongest: teacher, motivator, storyteller, or visionary.

Each of these voices has a strength and a weakness. Once you know this, you can leverage the strength and avoid the weakness, which will be a huge help in improving as a communicator. The best next step is to take the test. To access the test, go to JeffHenderson.com and click the link to "The Four Presenter Voices Assessment."

A Weekly Guide to
SOCIAL MEDIA

O ne of the most personable (and inexpensive) ways to show your community that your church or organization is FOR them is by engaging with them on social media. If we're not careful, we can simply talk about what's happening inside our organization and not what's happening outside in the community. At the For Company, we've developed a weekly guide that will put the *social* in social media. This will help you engage with your community in practical, personal ways. To download a PDF of this guide, visit JeffHenderson.com.

The Four for **FOR**
ASSESSMENT

The goal of any organization should be to close the gap between the two questions this book focuses on:

1. What do we *want* to be known FOR?
2. What *are* we known FOR?

When the answers to these two questions match, organizations harness the power of positive word-of-mouth advertising. The first step is to figure out where you are. As the old adage says, "Start where you are. Do what you can. Use what you have."

This survey has been developed to help you get the most value from the content of the book. It combines an assessment of your current situation and strategic questions to help you close the gap between the two key questions.

Who Should Complete this Survey

The survey is designed to be taken by key team members who are part of your organization. Ideally, those who complete the survey will first read *Know What You're FOR* to understand the ideas that are the basis for the questionnaire. There is value to be gained from all levels in the organization:

- **Leaders**—they are responsible for sharing vision/ purpose and for leading other team members.
- **Team members**—they experience being part of the organizational culture as well as interacting with customers and the community.
- **Other internal stakeholders**—this includes board members, donors, volunteers, and others who are a part of fulfilling the purpose of the organization.

Some of the questions in the survey require internal stakeholders (leaders and team members) to give their perceptions of the opinions of customers and community members. Their answers should draw on what they know from customer interaction and all of their experiences. Their responses to these questions are still valuable but must be evaluated with the understanding that they are putting themselves into the mind of the customer and making some assumptions.

Ideally, the organization should also obtain feedback on these issues from actual customers and community members.

To access the free link to the survey, visit JeffHenderson.com.

NOTES

1. Quoted in Patrick Salyer, "Listening to Social Media Cues Doesn't Mean Ceding Control," *Forbes*, August 4, 2012, www.forbes.com/sites/ciocentral/2012/08/04/listening-to-social-media-cues-doesnt-mean-ceding-control.
2. Jeff Henderson and Jan Smith, "031: World-Renowned Vocal Coach Jan Smith on Dreaming Big, Being Honest and Staying Humble," May 18, 2017, in *Launch Youniversity*, podcast, https://launchyouniversity.com/podcast/031-world-renowned-vocal-coach-jan-smith-dreaming-big-honest-staying-humble.
3. Henderson and Smith, "031: World-Renowned Vocal Coach Jan Smith."
4. See Don Tapscott, *The Digital Economy: Rethinking Promise and Peril in the Age of Networked Intelligence*, anniv. ed. (New York: McGraw Hill, 2014), http://dontapscott.com/books/digital-economy-anniversary-edition-2014.
5. Personal correspondence with Joey Reiman.
6. Ed Catmull, *Creativity, Inc.: Overcoming the Unseen Forces That Stand in the Way of True Inspiration* (New York: Random House, 2014), x.
7. See "Disney's FastPass: How an Employee-Innovator Made Magic Happen," Outthinker, November 29, 2016, https://outthinker.com/2016/11/29/disneys-fastpass-employee-innovator.

8. See Ken Blanchard, *Raving Fans: A Revolutionary Approach to Customer Service* (New York: Morrow, 1993).

9. Jeff Henderson, Kevin Jennings, and Eryn Eddy, "003: Eryn Eddy of So Worth Loving on Using Business to build Community," October 4, 2016, in *Launch Youniversity*, podcast, https://launchyouniversity.com/podcast/003-eryn-eddy-of-so-worth-loving-on-using-business-to-build-community.

10. See "Meaningful Brands 2017," Havas Group, https://dk.havas.com/wp-content/uploads/sites/37/2017/02/mb17_brochure_final_web.pdf.

11. "Meaningful Brands 2017," Havas Group, 2.

12. "Meaningful Brands 2017," Havas Group, 3.

13. Andy Stanley, *Deep and Wide: Creating Churches Unchurched People Love to Attend*, rev. ed. (Grand Rapids: Zondervan, 2016), 78.

14. Jeff Henderson, David Farmer, and Dana Spinola, "069: When Passion and Heart Lead the Way: Dana Spinola of fab'rik," March 22, 2018, in *Launch Youniversity*, podcast, https://launchyouniversity.com/podcast/069-when-passion-and-heart-lead-the-way-dana-spinola-of-fabrik.

15. Jeff Henderson and Sid Mashburn, "016: Sid Mashburn on Launching the Number One Men's Independent Clothing Store in the US Pt. 1," February 2, 2017, *Launch Youniversity*, podcast, https://launchyouniversity.com/podcast/016-sid-mashburn-launching-number-one-mens-independent-clothing-store-us-pt-1.

16. Cited in Andrew Cave, "Culture Eats Strategy for Breakfast: So What's for Lunch?" *Forbes*, November 9, 2017, www.forbes.com/sites/andrewcave/2017/11/09/culture-eats-strategy-for-breakfast-so-whats-for-lunch/#f0c80377e0fc.

17. Tim Irwin, *Extraordinary Influence: How Great Leaders Bring Out the Best in Others* (Hoboken, NJ: Wiley, 2018), 78; also visit www.extraordinaryinfluence.com.

18. Irwin, *Extraordinary Influence*, 87.

19. Irwin, *Extraordinary Influence*, 84.

20. Irwin, *Extraordinary Influence*, 81–93.

21. Quoted in Julia Pitt, "Steps to Success: The Value of Appreciation," *Royal Gazette*, May 7, 2013, www.royalgazette.com/article/20130507/COLUMN21/705079979.

22. See Stephen Covey, *The 7 Habits of Highly Effective People* (1979; repr., New York: Free Press, 2004), 150–60.

23. Andy Stanley and Frank Blake, "Vision: A Conversation with Frank Blake," September 2015, in *The Andy Stanley Leadership Podcast*, podcast, www.youtube.com/watch?v=FyfShcvL-Mc.

24. "Starbucks' Howard Schultz Doesn't Sleep—But Don't Blame the Coffee," *Here's the Thing*, September 27, 2016, www.wnycstudios.org/story/htt-howard-schultz.

25. Stanley and Blake, "Vision: A Conversation with Frank Blake."

26. Dr. Tim Irwin encourages CEOs to speak into these eight areas in the lives of those they work with: integrity, courage, humility, judgment, authenticity, self-regulation, wisdom, candor, resilience, and influence. When you see these personal qualities, let the celebrating begin. In one sense, it's hard to see these eight qualities on a spreadsheet, but the reality is that they do eventually show up—either in black or red.

27. For more on David, visit www.launchyouniversity.com.

28. Shane Benson, Chris Carneal, and Matthew Keller, "091: Creating the Culture You Want," August 22, 2018, in *Launch Youniversity*, podcast, https://launchyouniversity.com/podcast/091-creating-culture-want.

29. Quoted in David Griner, "As Domino's Expands Its Pothole Paving to All 50 States, Here's How to Bring It to Your Town," *Adweek*, August 29, 2018, www.adweek.com/creativity/as-dominos-expands-its-pothole-paving-to-all-50-states-heres-how-to-bring-it-to-your-town.

30. Roy Baumeister and Mark Leary, "The Need to Belong: Desire for Interpersonal Attachments as a Fundamental Human Motivation, *Psychological Bulletin* 117, no.3 (June 1995): 497–529. www.researchgate.net/publication/15420847_The_Need_to_Belong_Desire_for_Interpersonal_Attachments_as_a_Fundamental_Human_Motivation.

31. Tara Isabella Burton, "CrossFit Is My Church," *VOX*, September 10, 2018, www.vox.com/the-goods/2018/9/10/17801164/crossfit-soulcycle-religion-church-millennials-casper-ter-kuile.

32. Burton, "CrossFit Is My Church."

33. Phone interview with Kelly Thomas.

34. Danielle Martin, "A Neighborhood for Visalia," *Visalia Times-Delta*, May 18, 2017, www.visaliatimesdelta.com/story/news/local/2017/05/18/neighborhood-visalia/101859068.

35. "Our Business," Harley-Davidson, www.harley-davidson.com/us/en/about-us/company.html.

36. From a personal interview with Zim via email.

37. "Houston Grandfather Describes Jet-Ski Evacuation," https://abcnews.go.com/GMA/video/houston-grandfather-describes-jet-ski-evacuation-49509052.

38. A. J. Willingham, "The Remarkable Story behind This Harvey Jet Ski Rescue," *CNN*, August 31, 2017, www.cnn.com/2017/08/31/us/harvey-jet-ski-rescue-photo-trnd/index.html.

39. "Question and Answer with Joey Reiman, Author of *The Story of Purpose*," Wiley press release, January 11, 2013, www.wiley.com/WileyCDA/PressRelease/pressReleaseId-106041,descCd-release_additional_material.html.

40. Quoted in Jerry Glover, *Play to Win: Keys to Victory in the Game of Life* (Bloomington, IN: iUniverse, 2008), 55.

41. Marcus Buckingham, *Find Your Strongest Life: What the Happiest and Most Successful Women Do Differently* (Nashville: Thomas Nelson, 2009), 228.

42. Quoted in Earl Nightingale, "The Strangest Secret audio program," Nightingale Conant, www.nightingale.com/articles/the-strangest-secret.

43. Quoted in Gary Wolf, "Steve Jobs: The Next Insanely Great Thing," *Wired*, February 1, 1996, www.wired.com/1996/02/jobs-2.

44. Ryan Holiday, *Ego Is the Enemy* (New York: Penguin, 2016), 76–77, italics original.